This book is due for return on or before the last date shown below.

D1421555

BRINGING OUT THE DEAD
Paul Schrader

from the novel by Joseph Connelly

ff

faber and faber

First published in 2000
by Faber and Faber Limited
3 Queen Square London WC1N 3AU
Published in the United States by Faber and Faber, Inc.,
a division of Farrar, Straus and Giroux, Inc., New York

Photoset by Parker Typesetting Service, Leicester
Printed in England by Mackays of Chatham PLC, Chatham, Kent

Paul Schrader is hereby identified as author of this work
in accordance with Section 77 of the Copyright,
Designs and Patents Act 1988

*This book is sold subject to the condition that it shall not,
by way of trade or otherwise, be lent, resold, hired out or
otherwise circulated without the publisher's prior consent in
any form of binding or cover other than that in which it is
published and without a similar condition including this
condition being imposed on the subsequent purchaser*

A CIP record for this book
is available from the British Library

ISBN 0−571−20489−9

2 4 6 8 10 9 7 5 3 1

Cast List

FRANK PIERCE	Nicolas Cage
MARY BURKE	Patricia Arquette
LARRY	John Goodman
MARCUS	Ving Rhames
TOM WOLLS	Tom Sizemore
NOEL	Marc Anthony
NURSE CONSTANCE	Mary Beth Hurt
CY COATES	Cliff Curtis
DR HAZMAT	Nestor Serrano
NURSE CRUPP	Aida Turturro
ROSE	Cynthia Roman

MAIN CREW

Directed by	Martin Scorsese
Screenplay	Paul Schrader
From the novel by	Joe Connelly
Produced by	Barbara De Fina
	Scott Rudin
Co-Producers	Joseph P. Reidy
	Eric Steel
Executive Producers	Bruce S. Pustin
	Adam Schroeder
Original Music	Elmer Bernstein
Cinematography	Robert Richardson
Film Editing	Thelma Schoonmaker
Production Design	Dante Ferretti
Costume Design	Rita Ryack

A Paramount Pictures and Touchstone Pictures presentation

Bringing Out the Dead

I. EXT. NEW YORK STREET – NIGHT

An EMS 'bus' careens around a corner, tires squealing, lights flashing, siren whoop-whooping, swooping through the Stygian canyons of New York.

Frank Pierce, 30, drives. He wears dark cargo pants, black boots, a white shirt with the paramedic badge, 'EMS' gold logo on one collar, 'OPLM' on the other. 'Our Lady of Perpetual Mercy Paramedic' is inscribed in white across the back of his navy jacket. On his belt: two-way radio, leather gloves, beeper, drug kit, multi-purpose tool kit, mini-flashlight, collapsible baton.

Larry, 35, his partner for the night, overweight, sweating, rides techie (shotgun), both hands on the dash.

Frank scans the blurring cityscape for hidden danger. He is a young man of slight frame and an open face – his life, his possible futures, still before him: behind those open eyes, beneath those dark shadows, hollowness beckons.

Dispatcher's voice crackles through the cab static: 'Ladder 4, respond to a 10–22, four-flight residential, 417 West 32. 6–3 Boy, men's room Grand Central, man set his pants on fire. Bad burns. 7–7 David, at 177 West 24, there's woman who says a roach crawled in her ear. Can't get it out, says she's going into cardiac arrest . . .'

Frank's detached voice speaks over the urban landscape:

FRANK
(*V.O.*)

Thursday started out with a bang: a gunshot to the chest on a drug deal gone bad. Heat, humidity, moonlight – all the elements in place for a long weekend. I was good at my job: there were periods when my hands moved with a speed and skill beyond me and my mind worked with a cool authority I had never known. But in the last year I had started to lose that control. Things had turned bad. I hadn't saved anyone for months. I just needed a few slow nights, a week without tragedy followed by a couple of days off.

The radio continues: 'Zebra, 6–3Z –'

LARRY
(on radio)

We're there.

The ambulance brakes to a halt in front of a row of vintage walk-ups. Frank and Larry jump out: Frank lugs the EKG monitor (30 lbs) and airway bag, Larry the drug box, yellow oxygen pack slung over his shoulder. Neighbors crowd around.

OLD WOMAN
Which apartment? Which apartment?

FRANK
Move back. Where's the stairs? 5A.

NEIGHBOR WOMAN #1
Oh Jesus, it's Mr Burke.

The front door opens, a young boy holding it.

Author's note: in emergency situations, either on the street or in the hospital, it is assumed there is continual background noise – voices, sirens, cries, questions, etc.

CUT TO:

2. INT. TENEMENT STAIRWELL – NIGHT

Four flights up: Frank and Larry climbing rotting steps, gray-yellow painted walls, red doors with three locks each; Larry out of breath, his stomach rolling around like a bowling ball in a bag.

CUT TO:

3. INT. BURKE APARTMENT – NIGHT

They enter 5A. Mrs Burke, 55, her eyes run dry, standing in the center of the room, surrounded by neighbors. Someone leads them to the bedroom where Mr Burke, 60, lies unmoving, stretched out on the bed.

A young woman, Mary Burke, 24, kneels over the old man, pressing her lips to his flaccid mouth. John Burke, 30, grabs Frank's arm:

JOHN
We were just watching TV and Dad yelled out and started punching his chest, next thing he locked himself in the bathroom. I said we were gonna call you guys and he said not to. He was crying, I never heard him crying before, then he sorta stopped. We pulled him out and put him on the bed.

Frank and Larry moving the body to the floor:

FRANK
How long ago did he stop breathing?

JOHN
Maybe ten minutes. The woman on the phone tried to tell us how to do CPR. Please, you gotta do something.

FRANK
We'll do what we can.

Larry, sweating, ripping open Mr Burke's shirt, prepping electrode patches, hooking wires, Frank opening Burke's mouth, feeling a puff of gas escape; Larry calling for backup. Burke's EKG rhythm on the monitor a flat green line.

Frank's training takes over: he injects the long steel laryngoscope down Burke's throat, he finds a vein, injects epinephrine, followed by atropine, followed by another epi: no response on the monitor. Larry pulls out the paddles:

LARRY
Clear! Clear!

Larry activates defibrillator, shocks Burke. His daughter screams as the man's frail body leaps from the floor:

MARY
No more, please don't.

The green line still moves. Sweat drips from Larry's nose to Burke's chest. They shock him again. This time the body moves less. Frank glances up: Mr and Mrs Burke's wedding photo sits on the nightstand.

5

Other pictures: a day at the beach, a young serviceman, a bleeding-heart Christ, happy parents. Frank's mind drifts:

FRANK
(*V.O.*)

In the last year I had come to believe in such things as spirits leaving the body and not wanting to be put back, spirits angry at the awkward places death had left them. I understood how crazy it was to think this way, but I was convinced if I turned around, I'd see Old Man Burke standing at the window, watching, waiting for us to finish.

Frank feels Burke's heart beneath cracked ribs. The EKG remains flat. He's dead. It's time to quit.

FRANK
(*to Larry*)

I'll take over. Call ER and ask for an eighty-three.
(*to Mrs Burke*)

Sorry.

Larry stands, breathing heavy, looks for a phone. Frank turns to notice relatives and neighbors standing around.

FRANK

Do you have any music?

MARY

What?

FRANK

Music. I think it helps if you play something he liked.

MARY

John, play the Sinatra.

John enters crying. Mary repeats softly:

Play the Sinatra.

John exits. Frank notices Mary for the first time: blonde hair dyed black, cut short, loose-fitting tank dress, black make-up running down her cheeks. He notices her prom picture, glances back at Mary: it seems she hasn't smiled since that day six years before. Something special about her, that something that hits you right away.

6

'September of My Years' plays from the other room. Frank continues massaging Mr Burke's chest (now to Sinatra beat), even though it's hopeless. Larry returns:

LARRY

It's OK, Frank. We can call it. Eighty-three.

Frank feels something strange, looks into Burke's pupils, checks the neck pulse, wrist pulse. His eyes go to Larry:

FRANK

No we can't. He's got a pulse.

LARRY

No shit.

Larry checks the monitor: the green line up and down. Mary senses a change in status:

MARY

Is he going to be all right?

FRANK
(*not encouraging*)

His heart's beating.

A distant siren signals the arrival of backup. Frank turns to Larry:

FRANK

Have 'em bring up a stretcher.

He looks from Mary back to Mr Burke – breathing but comatose.

CUT TO:

4. INT. AMBULANCE – NIGHT

Larry climbing through the back doors, sitting in the jumpseat at the stretcher's head as Frank hangs IV bags, replugs EKG wires that have come loose.

Frank looks up, sees Mary entering; he takes her arm, turns her toward the rear doors:

FRANK

Help your family. Ride with your mother and brother.

7

She hesitates.

Help your family. They need you more. Help yourself.

Mary steps out, stands in the red flashing light as Larry closes the door, Frank climbs in the driver's seat.

CUT TO:

5. EXT. NINTH AVENUE – NIGHT

The EMS bus cruises up the avenue. Frank checks the side mirror: John, Mary and Mrs Burke pull behind in a black Ford. Seeing their faces in the rear-view mirror, Frank flips on the lights and sirens, hits the gas.

FRANK

(*off Larry's reaction*)

For the family.

Frank watches passing lights, cars, faces:

FRANK

(*V.O.*)

I needed to concentrate because my mind tended to wander on these short trips. It was the neighborhood I grew up in and where I had worked most as a paramedic and it held more ghosts per square foot than any other.

CUT TO:

6. EXT. OUR LADY OF PERPETUAL MERCY – NIGHT

Larry and Frank's 6–3 Zebra ambulance lined up beside two others outside a blazing 'Emergency' sign on the crowded side street.

CUT TO:

7. INT. MERCY ER – NIGHT

Every large city has a hospital Emergency Room so replete with trauma, violence and suffering it picks up the sobriquet 'Knife and Gun Club'. On Manhattan's West Side it's Our Lady of Perpetual Mercy, aka, Our Lady of Perpetual Misery.

ER: a white-lit cement box painted yellow and decorated with old framed playbills. Four rows of six plastic chairs face a TV bolted and chained to the ceiling. The seats are filled with backed-up drunks, assault victims and 'regulars', bleeding and spilling over against the walls and the floor, getting up to ask their status or going out to throw up and have a smoke.

Ramon, a particularly aggrieved regular, wakes up from a nap screaming for attention and – not receiving it – stumbles dramatically toward the triage desk, as if having a seizure.

Larry and Frank wheeling Burke in, two IV lines, each connected to an elbow, tangled in EKG cables. Two lacerated Russians scramble out of their way as they approach Griss, the large black sunglassed security guard. He looks up from his television guide:

GRISS

Hey, partner. Your man does not look well. They're not gonna appreciate you inside.

FRANK

Nobody loves me, Griss.

GRISS

Griss is only telling you things are backing up.

FRANK
(*pumping Ambu-bag*)

Griss, let us in.

GRISS

Whatever you say.

Griss pushes a button, activating the automatic door, striking the bandaged leg of a man lying down on a stretcher in the hall. Larry and Frank wheel Burke inside. A pleading family tries to follow. Griss stretches out his hand:

GRISS

You can't go in there, folks.

Mary, John and Mrs Burke rush in from the street, hoping some miracle has occurred during the drive to the hospital, approach the sign-in station.

Frank and Larry pass four stretchers lined against the wall – a passage nicknamed 'Skid Row', leading past triage Nurse Constance's station.

> **NURSE CONSTANCE**
> Just keep moving. Don't even slow down.

Nurse Constance turns back to the nervous man seated beside her:

> Sir, you say you've been snorting cocaine for three days and now you feel your heart is beating too fast and you would like us to help you. To tell the truth, I don't see why I should. If I'm mistaken, correct me. Did we sell you the cocaine? Did we push it up your nose?

Larry and Frank slow at the last Skid Row stretchers. On one, Noel, a young dark-skinned man with a chaotic mess of dreadlocks, pulls feverishly at his restraints:

> **NOEL**
> For God's sake, give me some water!

From the next stretcher a man with feet swollen purple like prize eggplants replies:

> **BIG FEET**
> Shut up! Goddamn civilians.

> **NOEL**
> Give me some water!

Nurse Crupp stops Frank and Larry as they approach the Critical Care room. Inside, the staff appears as if under siege by a battalion of shriveled men and women lying on a field of white sheets.

> **NURSE CRUPP**
> Don't take another step. We're on diversion. Can't accept any more patients. Your dispatcher should have told you.

> **FRANK**
> We got him at 49th and Tenth. You're closest.

> **NURSE CRUPP**
> Where will I put him, Frank? Look. Tell me.

FRANK

He wanted to come here. Said the nurses at Misery were the best.

NURSE CRUPP
(*acquiesces*)

All right, give me a minute. I'll kick someone out of slot three.

Larry unravels himself from the IV lines as a nurse walks over, takes Burke's pulse.

NOEL
(*to Frank*)

Excuse me. You are a very kind man. I can see that. A man like you could not refuse a poor sick dying helpless man a small cup of water.

FRANK

I can't. I have to stay with my patient.

BIG FEET

Shut the fuck up! If it wasn't for these dun feet I'd get up and kick your ass!

Dr Hazmat, 30, steps over to Burke:

HAZMAT

Godammit, guys, what are you doing to me? We're all backed up in here. Christ, would you look at him? He's gonna need the works. What's wrong with him?

LARRY

You should know. You pronounced him.

HAZMAT

You told me he was dead. Flatline.

FRANK

He got better.

HAZMAT

I hate pronouncing people dead over the phone.
(*flashes light in Burke's eyes*)

Better, huh? They're fixed and dilated. He's plant food.

NURSE CRUPP
(*returning*)
We stole a stretcher from X-ray. No pad on it, but I don't
think he'll mind. Put him in three, next to the overdose.

HAZMAT
He's our lowest priority now. He shouldn't even be here. All
this technology. What a waste.

Back at Security, the Burkes confront Griss.

GRISS
Please folks, step back.
(*they hesitate*)
Don't make me take off my sunglasses.

*In Critical Care, Larry wheels Burke into unit three as Dr Hazmat
turns Frank to face the room, explaining:*

HAZMAT
First-time heart attack, age forty-five. Should have gone to the
CCU ten hours ago. There's three bodies up there like the
one you just brought in. Over there, two AIDS patients, one
is twelve filling up with liquid. I'm gonna hafta intubate
because the kid's mother won't sign the Do Not Resuscitate.
Mercy killing doesn't translate well in Spanish. It's a sin to
tube this kid. Three more ODs from some new killer junk.
They call it Red Death.

*Hazmat pulls out a vial marked with a red skull and crossbones, shows
it to Frank.*

NOEL
Water, water, water, doctor man, water.

HAZMAT
A mix of heroin and I don't know what else, some kind of
amino acid maybe. Stuff so strong they're drinking it with
grain alcohol. You have to use ten times the usual amount of
Narcan and watch out when they wake up, liable to go nuts
on you.

FRANK
(*about Noel*)

He one of them?

HAZMAT

No, that's Noel. Used to be a regular off and on, hasn't been in in a while. He seized and almost coded – gave him a hypertonic solution. He drank so much the kidneys were taking out salt. One for the textbooks.

NOEL

Oh, Doctor, you are the greatest. You must help me.

BIG FEET

For God's sake, give him a drink of water.

HAZMAT

I am helping you, Noel. You could die if you drink more water.

Nurse Crupp pulls on Hazmat's arm.

HAZMAT

What is it?

She points to Burke. His monitor is ringing like a fire alarm. Hazmat and Crupp rush over, wave to others.

HAZMAT

Crupp, start CPR. Milagros, get me an epi. Odette, wake up Dr Stark. Tell him I need a blood gas, stat.

As the staff crowds around Burke, pulling the paddles from off the monitor, Frank, pushing his stretcher away. notices Big Feet climb on to his infected feet, hobble over, work to untie Noel.

NOEL

Bless you, sir, bless you.

BIG FEET

Shut up.

Frank heads down Skid Row pushing the stretcher, passing Nurse Constance speaking with a man with a gash over his eye:

NURSE CONSTANCE

... so you get drunk every day and you fall down. Tell me
why we should help you when you're going to get drunk
tomorrow and fall down again.

*Frank pushes the automatic door button – and is suddenly hit from
behind by Noel. The stretcher spins sideways. Noel, gown flapping,
tosses aside a six-year-old child, dives for the water fountain near the
statue of Our Lady, starts snorting water like a bull.*

MARY
(*to Frank*)

I *know* him. That's Noel.

Griss, seeing Noel and the fallen child, moves to take action.

FRANK

We'd better go outside. Quickly.

Frank and Mary step out into the humid night.

CUT TO:

8. EXT. MERCY EMERGENCY – NIGHT

*Checking behind them, Frank stops. The doors break open. Noel comes
flying out, bounces off the sidewalk. Griss, in the doorway, closes the
doors.*

Mary goes over to Noel:

MARY

Noel, Noel, it's me, Mary Burke. From 49th Street.

NOEL

Mary, Mary, Mary. I'm so thirsty. They won't give me
anything to drink. Please, Mary.

MARY
(*heading inside*)

I'll get you some.

*Frank watches: Mary returns with a cup of water, gives it to a grateful
Noel.*

FRANK

I wouldn't do that.

(*Noel drinks*)

The doctor seems to think he's suffering from some rare disorder.

MARY

It's not so rare. He grew up on our street. He's had a rough life, and he's a little crazy from it, but that's no excuse for not giving someone a lousy cup of water.

Mary starts to cry. Frank fumbles in his pocket, finds a tissue, gives it to her.

MARY

My father's dying, Noel.

NOEL

Oh Mary, Mary, Mary.

Noel hugs her clumsily, his shoulders bobbing. Frank watches, realizing that is what he should have done.

Noel releases Mary, walks off in his gown.

CUT TO:

9. EXT. NEW YORK STREETS – NIGHT

6–3 Zebra cruising down the avenue, Frank at the wheel, Larry shotgun.

LARRY

The Chinese close in five minutes. Beef lo mein. It's been on my mind since I woke. Whatjathink?

FRANK

I think the moment that food hits your mouth we'll get a job.

LARRY

Turn here. You missed it. The Chink is on 11th.

Frank turns, gets jammed up behind a pimp car at Tenth and 46th, a corner populated by pushers and hookers. Two whores stand in front of an abandoned building. Frank turns to look.

WHORE #1

Hey, ambulance man. What you looking at?

The second whore, wearing a yellow vinyl coat, turns. She has a face that instantly freezes Frank: the Rose face. Pregnant, she gestures to her belly:

WHORE #2

Pretty soon you'll be coming for me.

LARRY

Some partner you are, Frank. I coulda walked there faster. I'm starving and you stop to talk to hookers. You're making me nuts. Is that what you're trying to do, drag me down with you to nutsville?

Frank hits the whoop-whoop siren. The pimps in the black BMW jump, look back, realize it's only an ambulance, and pull away.

LARRY
(*slams dashboard*)

Oh no! – I just remembered.

FRANK

What?

LARRY

I'm so stupid. I had beef lo mein last night. I can't eat the same thing two nights in a row. It's almost two o'clock, what the hell am I gonna do? What you getting?

FRANK

I'm not hungry.

LARRY

Oh yeah, you don't eat food.

FRANK

I eat. I just haven't had coffee yet.

LARRY

Coffee and whiskey, lucky you ain't dead with that diet. Wait, I've got it. Half fried chicken with fries. Let's go, hurry up. Come on.

Frank speeds up the avenue. Noel, wearing generic homeless combat fatigues, muttering to his friends in Hell, passes on the sidewalk. Frank notices another hooker, catches her face, the same face as the pregnant Whore #2: the Rose face. *His mind drifts:*

FRANK

(*V.O.*)

Rose's ghost was getting closer. Ever since the call a month before, when I'd lost her, she seemed like all the girls in the neighborhood. One of the first things you learn is to avoid bad memories. I used to be an expert, but lately I'd found some holes. Anything could trigger it. It was as if something had clicked, a shutter had fallen in my brain, as if I had been watching a film and all of a sudden the soundtrack had failed.

All street noise abruptly ends.

The last month belonged to Rose, but there were a hundred more ready to come out.

CUT TO:

10. EXT. CHICKEN TAKE-OUT – NIGHT

The EMS vehicle is stopped at a fast-food joint. Larry orders, waits.

FRANK

(*V.O.*)

These spirits were part of the job. It was impossible to pass a building that didn't hold the ghost of something: the eyes of a corpse, the screams of a loved one. All bodies leave their mark. You cannot be near the newly dead without feeling it.

Larry gets his chicken, chats with counter clerk, returns.

I could handle that. What haunted me now was more savage: spirits born half-finished, homicides, suicides, overdoses, innocent or not, accusing me of being there, witnessing a humiliation which they could never forgive.

Larry climbs in, sets his take-out on the dash, hands Frank a coffee as a walkie-talkie squawks.

> **LARRY**
>
> Turn it off.

> **FRANK**
>
> What?

> **LARRY**
>
> You know what. The radio.

> **FRANK**
>
> That's not the police band. That's your fire department scanner. In your bag.

> **LARRY**
>
> Oh.

Larry reaches into his all-purpose canvas bag, pulls out the scanner. As he reaches to turn it off, it squawks:

> **POLICE DISPATCH**
>
> Ladder Four, respond to a 10–22 six-flight residential, 534 West 32nd.

> **LARRY**
>
> Let's do it. It might be a good one.

> **FRANK**
>
> There are no good fires. People die in fires. People get burned up in fires. People can't breathe.

> **LARRY**
>
> That's what we're here for. Let's go, Frank.

Larry prepares to key a response. Frank reaches over, grabs the radio antenna.

> **FRANK**
>
> Don't push it, Larry.

They tug-of-war over the radio like two schoolkids.

> **LARRY**
>
> You're burned out. You're scorched.

FRANK

Not yet, Larry, I'm still burning and if you get any closer I'll put a burn on you.

The EMS Dispatcher interrupts their argument:

RADIO DISPATCHER

Six–three Zebra. Zebra three, I need you.

LARRY

You see, he's giving it to us anyway.

RADIO DISPATCHER

Zebra, are you there? I'm holding an unconscious at Ninth and 41st.

They release the fire scanner.

LARRY
(*screams*)

No! It's three o'clock. That can only mean one thing.

FRANK

Mr Oh.

LARRY

It's Mr Oh. I'm not answering it.

RADIO DISPATCHER

Answer the radio, Zebra. You know it's that time.

LARRY

Four times this week I've had him. Aren't there any other units out there? Don't answer the radio. They'll give it to someone else.

RADIO DISPATCHER

Sixty-three Zebra. Six–three Zebra. You're going out of service in two minutes.

Pause. Neither moves.

LARRY

Look, Frank, when I say don't answer it, that means answer it.

> (*picks up the mike*)

You can do that for me at least.

> (*keys mike*)

Six–three Zebra.

RADIO DISPATCHER

Yes, Zebra. You'll be driving to the man who needs no introduction, chronic caller of the year three straight and shooting for number four. The duke of drunk, the king of stink, our most frequent flyer, Mr Oh.

LARRY

Ten–four.

> (*Frank starts the engine*)

Don't go. Not this time.

FRANK

> (*driving off*)

Relax, it's a street job, easy except for the smell. We'll just throw him in back and zip over to Mercy – no blood, no dying, that's how I look at it. He's just a drunk.

LARRY

It's not our job to taxi drunks around.

FRANK

They'll just keep calling.

LARRY

Someone's gonna die some day 'causa that bum, going to have a cardiac and the only medics will be taking care of Mr Oh.

CUT TO:

11. EXT. STREET CORNER – NIGHT

Frank and Larry standing over Mr Oh, 40, surrounded by street people. Oh lays curled up beside his wheelchair, wearing a black garbage bag with holes cut out for his arms, his pants around his knees.

MALE STREET PERSON #1

He's bad, mister. He ain't eaten nuthin all day, he's seizing and throwing up.

Larry, holding his nose as he speaks:

LARRY
So what's different about him today?

MALE STREET PERSON #1
He says his feet hurt.

LARRY
(*mock concerned*)
Why didn't you say so? Let's go.

MALE STREET PERSON #1
(*reaching down*)
I can't find a pulse, but he's still breathing.

FRANK
Looks like we're just in time. Would you step aside, sir?

LARRY
He's drunk.

MALE STREET PERSON #1
He's sick. You gotta help him.

LARRY
He's fine. He can walk to the hospital.

FEMALE STREET PERSON
Walk? You crazy? He's in a wheelchair.

LARRY
Don't start that. I've seen him walk. He walks better than me.

Frank crouches over Oh, tries to pull Oh's pants over his white, dirt-stained ass. Oh moans:

MR OH
Oh, oh, oh.

LARRY
That's him, Mr Oh.
(*pulls at his arm*)
Get up. He's walkin' this time.

Larry and Frank get Oh to his feet only to have him stumble over his lowered trousers. This time Frank lifts him, sets his white ass cheeks into the wheelchair. They push him toward the ambulance.

CROWD

Good luck! Get better!

CUT TO:

12. EXT. NEW YORK STREET — NIGHT

6–3 Zebra heads up the avenue, double Caduceus symbols shining from the back of the van.

Inside the cab, Larry and Frank lean out the front windows to avoid the king of stink:

LARRY

Faster! God!

FRANK
(*flips on top lights*)

Faster!

CUT TO:

13. INT. MERCY ER — NIGHT

Griss holding up his hand:

GRISS

Get that stinky-assed motherfucking bug-ridden skell out of my face.

Frank and Larry stand beside Oh slumped in his wheelchair. Fellow drunks welcome their comrade from plastic chairs. Nurse Constance escorts a young man from the triage area:

NURSE CONSTANCE

... I would have to register you to give you something to eat and my conscience just will not allow that. Griss, this gentleman wants to leave.
(*looks at Oh*)
He looks pale. You're not eating enough. You need more fibre.

Griss shows the young man the door.

> **LARRY**
> (*holds up his report*)
> He's wasted. That's my diagnosis: shit-faced.

> **NURSE CONSTANCE**
> He just needs a bath and some food. Take him in back and
> see if you can find a stretcher.

> **LARRY**
> (*to Frank*)
> She's nuts. That's why he comes here. She encourages him.

Griss returns as Crupp calls from Critical Care area:

> **NURSE CRUPP**
> Don't you dare! That's my last stretcher. This is not a
> homeless shelter. He'll have to wait in the lobby.

> **GRISS**
> No way, man. Not even in the corner. Griss cannot abide the
> funk tonight.

Larry and Frank turn and wheel Mr Oh outside.

CUT TO:

14. EXT. MERCY EMERGENCY – NIGHT

*Larry setting Oh outside the entrance, heading towards the all-night
deli. Frank takes out a cigarette.*

*Mary Burke walks up the drive opening a pack of cigarettes. Frank
offers her a light. She inhales, exhales:*

> **MARY**
> It's my first cigarette in over a year.

> **FRANK**
> The first is always the best.

> **MARY**
> It's the waiting that's killing me, not knowing, you know. It's
> really hard on my mother. The doctor doesn't think my

23

father'll make it. He says he was dead too long, after six minutes the brain starts to die and once that goes, close the door.

FRANK

You never know.

MARY

I mean if he was dead, I could handle that.

FRANK

At least he's got people around him.

MARY

I'm not so sure. My father and I haven't spoken in three years. When my brother called to say my father was having a heart attack, that he'd locked himself in the bathroom, all the way going over I was thinking how I was gonna tell him what a bastard he was. Then when I got up the stairs and we moved him on to the bed, I thought of all the other things I wanted to say.

FRANK

Even when you say the things, there's always more things.

MARY

Right now, I'm more worried about my mother than anything. They won't let her see my father.

FRANK

Go home. Take her home. Get some rest. Not going to find anything out now.

MARY

That's what I told her. If she could just seen him for a second, then I could take her home.

Larry walks back with a coffee for himself and a brown bag beer for Frank.

LARRY

Here's yar dinner. Time to switch. I wheel, you heal.

CUT TO:

*4:00 am. The EMS vehicle drives downtown. The city has transformed:
a deserted city, inhabited by the hardcore: hardcore nightshift employees,
hardcore party-goers, hardcore druggies, hardcore homeless, people with
something special to do or nowhere to go.*

> RADIO DISPATCHER
>
> Six–two David on the corner of Thirty-eight and Two you'll
> find a three-car accident, two taxis and a taxi. Six–two Henry,
> 487 West Two–two, report of a very bad smell. No further
> information . . .

*Larry driving at a good clip, riding both the gas and the brake pedals,
enjoying the newfound freedom of movement.*

> FRANK
>
> Larry, swing over to Tenth. We're gonna hafta run one of
> these calls.

> LARRY
>
> Relax, will you?

Frank places both hands on the dash as Larry squeals around a corner.

> FRANK
> (V.O.)
>
> The biggest problem with not driving is that whenever there's
> a patient in back you're also in the back. The doors close,
> you're trapped. Four in the morning is always the worst time
> for me, just before dawn, just when you've been lulled into
> thinking it might be safe to close your eyes for one minute.
> That's when I first found Rose . . .

*Larry slows down on a side street. Frank turns to watch a homeless man.
The man looks back: it's Rose. The Rose face. Soundtrack cuts off.*

> She was on the sidewalk, not breathing.

Frank turns to Larry:

> FRANK
>
> I'm not feeling very well, Larry. I say we go back to the
> hospital and call it a night.

LARRY

You have no sick time, Frank. No time of any kind. Everyone knows that.

FRANK

Take me back, put me to bed; I surrender. We've done enough damage tonight.

LARRY

You take things too seriously. Look at us, we're cruising around, talking, taking some quiet time, getting paid for it. We've got a good job here.

FRANK

Yeah, you're right.

Larry pulls on to a pier on West 13th Street by the river, slows to a stop. Larry cuts the lights, not bothering to inform his partner what he already knows: they're taking a rest.

CUT TO:

16. EXT. PIER 54 – NIGHT

6–3 Zebra sits in the quiet dark. Larry puffs a cigarette.

FRANK

Tell me, you ever think of doing anything else?

LARRY

Sure. I'm taking the captain's exam next year. After the kids are in school, Louise can go back to the post office and I thought, what the hell, I'll start my own medic service. Out on the Island the volunteers are becoming salaried municipal. It's just a matter of time and who you know. Someday it's going to be Chief Larry calling the shots.

Larry tosses the cigarette out the window, leans against the door jamb, closes his eyes. In a second he's asleep.

Frank turns down the radio volume: the calls are fewer and further between now. Frank leans back, tries to rest:

FRANK
(*V.O.*)

I'd always had nightmares, but now the ghosts didn't wait for me to sleep. I drank every day. Help others and you help yourself, that was my motto, but I hadn't saved anyone in months. It seemed all my patients were dying. I'd waited, sure the sickness would break, tomorrow night, the next call, the feeling would drop away. More than anything else I wanted to sleep like that, close my eyes and drift away . . .

TIMECUT: *Radio wakes Frank from his reverie.*

RADIO DISPATCHER

Zebra. Six–three Zebra.
(*Frank opens eyes*)
Zebra, answer the radio. Come on, I've got one for you. Pick up the radio and push the button on the side and speak into the front.

FRANK
(*answering call*)

Zebra.

RADIO DISPATCHER

Male bleeding, corner of 44th and Eighth. No further information.

FRANK

Ten–four.

Frank hangs up, bangs Larry's steering-wheel:

FRANK

We have a call, Chief. Somebody's bleeding, 44th and Eighth.

Larry, instinctively reaches for the ignition key, starts the engine, drops the ambulance into gear, hits the lights, jerks the EMS bus away, still half-asleep.

CUT TO:

17. EXT. 44TH AND EIGHTH – NIGHT

6–3 Zebra coming to a bone-jarring stop at the corner. Getting out of the techie seat, Frank sees Noel, his face bloody, charging at him.

NOEL

Kill me!

Noel has sliced up a tire and fastened the pieces with string over his shoulders. Tin cans circle his wrists and ankles. One hand carries a broken bottle, the other a stringless violin.

Frank jumps back inside as Noel rams the window, leaving stains from his blood-matted dreadlocks. Larry calls for backup: medics, police, firemen, anybody.

The side-window glass bends as Noel rams his head against it. Frank reaches for the short club between the seats; Noel holds the jagged bottle to his neck.

FRANK

Noel, don't!

Noel drops the bottle. Frank rolls down the window.

LARRY

He's crazy.

FRANK

You think so?

NOEL

See, I can't do it. I came out of the desert. I was left to die in the sun.

FRANK

You came out of the hospital. You were tied down and hallucinating. You got some bad chemicals in your head, Noel. There's some medicine at the hospital that will fix that.

NOEL

No, no medicine!

Noel swings his bloody dreadlocks: Frank ducking, getting splattered anyway, rolling up the window.

He got you.

A black punk calls from the crowd:

BLACK PUNK

Do it! Man wants to die. Take him out. I know how to kill
that mother.
    (*points a finger*)
Pop, pop.

*Noel, spraying blood, chases the punk. The crowd scatters. Noel runs
into the street and lays down in traffic. Frank, carrying the short bag,
gets out, walks over, hunches beside Noel:*

FRANK

Noel, you didn't let me finish. We have rules against killing
people on the street. It looks bad. But there's a special room
at the hospital for terminating. A nice quiet room with a big
bed.

NOEL

Oh man, do you mean that?
    (*smiles*)
Thank you, man, thank you. How? How do you kill me?

FRANK

Well, you have a choice: pills, injection or gas.

A siren draws closer. Noel gets to his feet as Larry opens the rear doors.

NOEL

I think pills. Yes, pills, definitely.

*A second ambulance skids to a stop. Tom Wolls, 35, a 220-pound
balding bruiser, gets out in a continuous motion.*

LARRY

Jesus, Tom Wolls. That crazy motherfucker.

FRANK

Used to be my partner.

Frank sidesteps Wolls' backslap.

WOLLS

Frank, this the guy you called about? I know him.
(*pushes Noel*)
You give my friend here any trouble and I'll kill you.

NOEL
(*smiles*)

Yes, at the hospital.

WOLLS

This looks like a very bad man I took in a couple weeks ago, a man who'd been holding two priests hostage with a screwdriver. I told him if I ever caught him making trouble again I'd kick the murdering life outta him.

FRANK

It's not worth it, Tom. He's surrendering.

WOLLS

No prisoners. Don't worry, Frank, just a little psychological first aid.

Wolls hauls back, swings at Noel; Noel ducks. Grunt, Wolls' partner, watches from the driver's seat.

WOLLS

Stay still, dammit!

Wolls throws Noel against the bus, knocks him down, sets to kicking him.

FRANK

Don't do it, Tom!

Noel moans. Larry sticks his head out the back of the bus:

LARRY

There's a double shooting three blocks down. Eighth and 41st. Confirmed.

WOLLS
(*looking up*)

We'll do it.

FRANK

Let go of him.

Wolls releasing Noel as Noel scrambles into the bus, Frank stepping over him, Larry climbing into the driver's seat, Frank closing the doors. Noel trembles:

NOEL

At the hospital. You told me at the hospital.

Larry squeals off full gun, all sirens blaring: the Wah, the Yelp, the Super Yelp. Strobe bar, side strobes, quarter panel strobes. Rock 'n' Roll.

CUT TO:

18. EXT. EIGHTH AND 41ST – NIGHT

Both EMS buses braking to a stop at the crime scene, cops holding the crowd back; Wolls, Frank, Larry, Grunt moving through the crowd.

FRANK & WOLLS

EMS. Move it!

BYSTANDER

Man just walked up and shot 'em. Not a word. Man, that was cold.

Two boys, drug dealers, lie bleeding on the sidewalk. Frank drops to his knees beside one, Wolls the other. Larry wheels out the stretcher. Frank checks the pulse.

FRANK

(*to drug dealer*)

Where you hit?

VOICE IN THE CROWD

Outlaw did this. He works for Cy.

DRUG DEALER

Look at that shit. He put a hole in me, man.

Two white vials roll out of the drug dealer's shirt: they are marked with red skull and crossbones. Frank looks over – they're gone, swiped by eager hands.

Listening for a heartbeat, Frank calls to Wolls:

31

FRANK

Major Tom, I'm going to Misery. You take yours to Bellevue.

WOLLS

OK, you take yours to heaven. I'll take mine to hell.
(*looks up*)
C'mon, Grunt, let's move 'em out.

CUT TO:

19. INT. 6–3 ZEBRA EMS VEHICLE – NIGHT

Larry charging through the night, while in back, Frank, wraps a tourniquet around the drug dealer's arm: he's dying fast.

FRANK

You're gonna feel a stick in your arm. Don't move.

DRUG DEALER

I'm quittin'. I'm going in the Army where it's safe. I don't want to die.

NOEL

I want to die. I'm the one.

FRANK

You're not going to die.

NOEL

What did you say?

FRANK
(*to Noel*)
Shut up. You're going to die and he's not. Got it?

DRUG DEALER
(*weak*)

Hold my hand.

FRANK

I can't. I got to do the other arm.

DRUG DEALER

Please. Just hold my hand, man.

FRANK
(*to Noel*)
Hold this – right there. If you let go, I swear, I won't kill you.

Noel holds the IV bag as Frank searches for a vein, inserts second IV needle.

CUT TO:

20. EXT. MERCY EMERGENCY – NIGHT

Larry pulls into Our Lady of Perpetual Mercy Emergency. Frank says to the boy:

FRANK
It's all right. We're here.

No answer. Frank feels for a pulse, listens with the stethoscope: nothing. Larry opens the doors. Frank jumps out, Noel is bent over the boy holding him.

LARRY
Noel, let's go.

Frank tries to pull the stretcher out. Noel jumps out, knocking Larry back, and runs into the street.

FRANK
He's not breathing. Call a code.

Larry and Frank pull the dead boy out of the bus.

CUT TO:

21. INT. MERCY ER – NIGHT

Frank finishes his report, hands a copy to the clerk, looks around the now almost empty waiting area. John Burke sleeps slumped in one of the chairs. Griss stands at his post.

Marcus and Stanley, fellow EMS paramedics, veteran and trainee, stand drinking coffee, waiting for paperwork.

MARCUS
. . . there's something jammed in his teeth. These junkies, of

course, none of them wants mouth-to-mouth; it was a
blow-drier, I pulled it out. The man was cold, 'cept for his
throat – they musta been blow-drying it for an hour. Second-
degree burns of the tongue.

STANLEY

You ever do mouth-to-mouth?

MARCUS

A long time ago, when I was starting out like you. Never
again, kid. Chances are you end up with a mouthful of puke.

STANLEY

I would if I had to. It's part of the job.
(*to Frank*)

What about you?

FRANK

Once, on a baby.

Griss, listening in, interjects:

GRISS

Oh, babies. Babies are a whole different thing entirely.

*Frank nods to Griss in agreement, says goodbye to Marcus and Stanley.
Pulling out a pack of cigarettes, he steps outside.*

CUT TO:

22. EXT. MERCY EMERGENCY – NIGHT

*Frank exits, lights up. The sky is going blue. Larry, beside 6–3 Zebra,
sheets wrapped around his legs, torso and arms, duct-tapes the sheets to
gloves at his wrists. He grabs a mop and jumps into the bloody interior
of the ambulance, goes to work.*

*Mary Burke, weary, steps up beside Frank. He offers a cigarette. She
accepts:*

MARY

You shouldn't smoke.

FRANK

It's okay. They're prescription.

(*beat*)

Works better with a little whiskey.

MARY

That's my brother's problem. He's passed out inside.

Larry jumps theatrically out of the ambulance, swings the mop wildly over his head:

LARRY

That's it! I can't do it any more!

Mary laughs once, less than a second. She notices bloodstains on Frank's shirt:

MARY

That boy you brought in, he was shot, wasn't he?

FRANK

Yes.

MARY

He's dead, huh?

FRANK

Yes.

MARY
(*pause*)

I think this place stinks.

FRANK

Our Lady of Misery.

MARY

Did you see my father?

FRANK

No.

MARY

It's crazy in there. What's wrong with that doctor? He keeps mumbling, poking himself in the eye when he talks to me.

FRANK

He's working a double shift.

35

MARY

Thing is, I'm supposed to be the fuckup. The one on the stretcher in there – that's supposed to be me. With my parents crying out here. A lot of guilt, you know what I mean?

He does.

My father's in a coma, now my mother's going crazy. It's like she's in a trance.

FRANK

She should go home.

MARY

I'd take her, but then who would stay here?

Frank looks at her, trying to say the right thing. He notices Mrs Burke coming from inside.

FRANK

Here she is.

Mrs Burke, dazed, steps out. They join her.

MRS BURKE

It wasn't him.

MARY

You saw him?

MRS BURKE

They showed me someone. It wasn't him. It wasn't my husband.

FRANK

Mrs Burke, please, they'll take care of him. You should go home now.

MRS BURKE

I should know my own husband. They wouldn't let me see him.

She drifts away. Frank speaks to Mary:

FRANK

Larry and I'll drop her back home. Help me get her to the ambulance.

MRS BURKE
You want some coffee? I have some apple sauce cake too.

They walk Mrs Burke to 6–3 Zebra. Mrs Burke attempts to sit on the back bumper of the EMS vehicle; Frank puts her inside.

MARY

Thank you.

Mary watches as Larry backs up the EMS vehicle, Frank sitting in the back with her mother, and pulls into first light.

CUT TO:

23. EXT. FRANK'S STREET CORNER – EARLY MORNING

Larry dropping Frank off at the corner of his street, driving on.

It is as if the sun has risen on a different city, different from the one which Frank drove through the night before: a city of crumbling neighborhoods laid bare by sunlight; a city of day people, getting up, having breakfast, going to work.

CUT TO:

24. INT. FRANK'S APARTMENT – DAY

*Frank's studio apartment betrays a minimal existence: single bed, table, fridge and stove, loveseat, bookshelf, television. The bookshelf contains a CD player, medical texts, old schoolbook (*Romantic Poetry*), paperback novels and, incongruously, a picture book of women's fashion.*

A framed commendation from the New York Fire Department hangs beside an open closet of work clothes, corduroy jacket, two ties on a hook. Remnants of a fast-food breakfast on the table. Aluminum foil covers the windows, blocking out the sunlight.

Frank stands bareback at a single open window, smoking, drinking from a glass of whiskey, looking across the gray cityscape of high rises and water tanks: winding down from a night's work:

FRANK
(*V.O.*)

Saving someone's life is like falling in love, the best drug in the world. For days, sometimes weeks afterwards, you walk the street making infinite whatever you see. Once, for a few weeks I couldn't feel the earth. Everything I touched became light. Horns played in my shoes; flowers fell from my pockets . . .

TIME DISSOLVES: *Frank paces the room. Pours himself another drink.*

You wonder if you've become immortal, as if you saved your own life as well. What was once criminal and happenstance suddenly makes sense. God has passed through you, why deny it: that for a moment there, why deny for a moment there, God was you.

TIME DISSOLVES: *window is closed. Frank tosses in his sleep.*

Taking credit when things go right doesn't work the other way. When things go wrong, spreading the blame is an essential medic survival tool: the family was crazy, the equipment broke, the patient smelled. The God of Hellfire is not a role anyone wants to play.

Nightstand alarm buzzes. Frank sits up, looks at the clock. Stretching his neck, he walks over to the sink, runs water on his hands and face.

CUT TO:

25. EXT. EMS GARAGE – NIGHT

The maintenance garage and dispatch office adjacent to Our Lady of Perpetual Mercy. (Frank may walk through.)

CUT TO:

26. INT. EMS GARAGE OFFICE – NIGHT

Frank standing on one foot before the desk of Captain Barney, 50, ex-paramedic and lifetime civil servant.

FRANK

Good morning, Captain.

Captain Barney looks over to Miss Williams, his secretary, seated at a desk perpendicular to his:

CAPTAIN BARNEY

What am I going to do with this guy?
(*to Frank*)
Pierce, I was just on the phone with Borough Command. Out of twelve shifts this month, you've been late for nine, sick four and that includes the shift where you came late and went home early.

FRANK

I'm sick. That's what I've been telling you.

CAPTAIN BARNEY

You're killing me, you know that? You got no sick time according to Command. I've been told to terminate.

FRANK

It's OK. I'll just get my things out of my locker.

CAPTAIN BARNEY

I've never fired anyone in my life.

FRANK

I'm sorry, Captain. Don't take it too hard.

CAPTAIN BARNEY

Nobody tells me to fire anyone. I told them shove it up the big one.
(*looks at Miss Williams*)
Sorry.
(*back to Frank*)
I said, you want to fire him, come over and do it yourself.

FRANK

You know they won't do it. It's up to you. You gotta be strong.

CAPTAIN BARNEY

I feel for you, but we got an emergency here. It's a weekend of full moons. Everyone's called in sick. Larry, Veeber, Stanley too. We need bodies out there. I had to put Marcus on 6–2 Young. You know he's not supposed to work two nights in a row.

> FRANK

You swore you'd fire me if I came in late again.

> CAPTAIN BARNEY

I'll fire you tomorrow. Hell, better than that, I'll forward you some sick time. A week, two weeks off – how about that?

> FRANK

I don't think a week's gonna do it.

> CAPTAIN BARNEY

I'm sorry, Pierce.
> *(hands Frank keys)*
You're going out with Marcus. Duty calls. The city needs you.

CUT TO:

27. EXT. NEW YORK STREET – NIGHT

6–2 Young heading downtown, lights off, slowing down for cross streets. At the wheel: Marcus, 40, black, reserved, chin erect, seeming too old for the job.

Frank, riding techie, looks out the window: they pass Sister Fetus, a thirtyish ranting Dominican street preacher. She wears a backwards baseball cap covered with enamel pins, a faded T-shirt ('It's Ten o'Clock, Do You Know Where Jesus Is?'). She has earned her name by the fact that she wears, around her neck, hung from a chain, a painted plaster cast of an unborn fetus, much like those used in anti-abortion displays. She speaks to no one in particular.

> MARCUS

My Lord, mother man, you look like hell. What were you drinking?

> FRANK

The captain almost fired me tonight. I'm on my way out. Any time now.

MARCUS

Nobody gets fired. Look at me. Only thing they might do is transfer you to the Bronx. You look like you aged ten years since I rode with you last.

FRANK

I ain't feeling so hot. I've been seeing the ghosts –

MARCUS

You mean people we lost?

FRANK

Yeah.

MARCUS

Ever notice people who see shit always are crazy?

FRANK

I think the worst is over.

MARCUS

It can always get worse. You can't change what's out there, only where you're coming from. You got to let the Lord take over, in here.

(*points to Frank's chest*)

Love, a black, tough-talking female dispatcher, comes on the radio:

DISPATCHER LOVE

Six–two Young.

(*beat*)

Let's go, Six–two Young. Answer the radio.

FRANK

Hey, Marcus, it's Love. I haven't heard her in months.

MARCUS

She only works when I'm on. I make her wait and it drives her crazy.

FRANK

Is it true that you and Love went on a blind date?

(*Marcus looks away*)

She hit you with a bottle?

41

MARCUS

She loves me the way no woman ever has.

DISPATCHER LOVE

Six–two Young, I don't have time for your games. Now
answer me or do I have to come out there myself?

MARCUS

I usually don't do calls before coffee. But I think it might do
you some good.
                    (*picks up mike*)
Six–two Young is here and I'm gonna take care of you, baby.
Don't you worry about a thing, yahear, cause Marcus is alive
and on arrival.

DISPATCHER LOVE

I'm not your baby, Young, I'm not your mother either.
You're going to a cardiac arrest, 30th and eleventh, northeast
corner. It's a club. Take the back entrance.

MARCUS

Ten–four, hon.
                    (*to Frank*)
You feel better, Frank?

FRANK

I feel worse.

MARCUS

That's good, man. I'm doing this for you.

Marcus flips on the lights and siren.

CUT TO:

28. EXT. 30TH AND ELEVENTH – NIGHT

*Marcus grabs the yellow airway bag, leaving Frank to lug the three
heavier pieces as they push their way through the usual crowd of
models and wrestlers toward a black jacketed doorman holding a
walkie-talkie:*

MARCUS
(*to crowd*)
I hope we're not too late from you guys holding us up here.

CUT TO:

29. INT. CLUB BACKSTAGE — NIGHT

The doorman leads Frank and Marcus through the smoky graffiti-covered backstage anterooms to a cubicle where a knot of club types and band members hover around I. B. Bangin, 18-year-old white rapper, face up, blank-eyed and breathless on dirt-impacted carpet. Hip-hop music echoes from the club PA.

Frank kneels beside I. B. Bangin, taking a pulse, realizing it's the gray and black stage make-up making him seem DOA. He pulls up I. B. Bangin's eyelid, shines a light into the pupil.

MARCUS
OK, what happened?

DRUMMER
He's going to be all right, isn't he?

MARCUS
No. He's dead.

DRUMMER
No way, man. We just got our first deal.

MARCUS
He's dead and there's nothing we can do. Come on, Frank, that's it.

FRANK
(*whispers*)
He's not dead. It's a heroin overdose. Break out the Narcan.

MARCUS
(*announcing*)
He's dead unless you folks want to stop bullshitting me and tell it straight. Then, Lord willing, we'll try to bring him back.

A bystander, actually a bylayer, in that he's lying under the radiator, speaks up:

43

BYSTANDER

He broke up with his old lady.

GIRLFRIEND

We didn't break up. We're just seeing other people.

MARCUS

I'm still waiting and this young man is still dead.

BYSTANDER

She broke his heart.

The girlfriend shoots a look at the bystander. Marcus just stands, hands on hips, silent. Frank opens the drug box.

The drummer relents:

DRUMMER

All right, all right, he's been snorting that Red Death stuff. Been going for four days.

MARCUS
(*brings hands together*)

What's his name?

DRUMMER

I. B. Bangin.

MARCUS

What'd you mean I. B. Bangin? What kind of name is I. B. Bangin?

DRUMMER

I don't know his real name.

GIRLFRIEND
(*hesitant*)

It's Frederick. Frederick Smith.

MARCUS
(*to body*)

Okay, Freddy.

GIRLFRIEND

It's Frederick.

MARCUS

Okay, I. B. Bangin, we're gonna bring you back. Every person
here grab the hand of the person next to you.

*Marcus assists the crowd – some have difficulty finding each other's
hands – as Frank breaks the cellophane off a syringe, locates a vial of
Narcan. Marcus looks at Frank, waiting for the signal.*

*Frank wraps I. B. Bangin's arm, finds a vein, poises the syringe, gives
Marcus the thumbs-up sign. Marcus responds by raising his hands:*

MARCUS

Oh, Lord, here I am again to ask one more chance for a
sinner. Bring back I. B. Bangin, Lord. You have the power,
the might, the super light, to spare this worthless man.

*Frank injects I. B. Bangin: he responds to the Narcan with a jolt,
opening his eyes, raising his hands.*

GIRLFRIEND
(kneeling)

Frederick!

BYSTANDER

Oh wow, man. Oh wow.

MARCUS

Rise, I. B. Stand and start your new life.

I. B. BANGIN
(sick)

What happened?

GIRLFRIEND

You died, you stupid bastard. I warned you.

DRUMMER

You guys are awesome.

FRANK
(to I. B. Bangin)

C'mon.

*Frank and the Girlfriend guide I. B. Bangin to the door as Marcus
collects the gear.*

Not us. The first step is Love. The second is Mercy.

He follows Frank, I. B. Bangin and Girlfriend out, calling for the crowd to clear.

CUT TO:

30. INT. MERCY ER – NIGHT

I. B. Bangin sitting with Nurse Constance in triage. Past Griss, Frank talks with Dr Hazmat:

FRANK

That guy I brought in yesterday, post-cardiac arrest. He's gone.

HAZMAT

Burke. You won't believe it. He's showing cognitive signs. He started with spontaneous respiration, now he's fighting to pull out the tube. Had to sedate him. He's in a CAT scan. There's no room in ICU, so I'm giving him every test I can: thrombolytics, steroids, nitrodrips, heparin.

FRANK

What do you think?

HAZMAT

Who knows? It's all lower-brain-stem activity. The heart refuses to stabilize – he's coded eleven times since he got here. This guy's a fighter. Every time the Valium wears off, he starts yanking those restraints.

FRANK

The family know?

HAZMAT

I wanted to bring them in, to see if he'd respond to voices, but they weren't in the waiting room. The guy's daughter was in my face all last night and when I finally have something positive to tell her, she's gone.

Frank nods, walks down Skid Row, passing Nurse Constance lecturing I. B. Bangin:

> NURSE CONSTANCE
>
> . . . you put poison in your veins and now that you're breathing again you can't wait to say thank you and go back to poison shopping. Well, since we saved your life, maybe you could do us a favor and stop breathing in another city next time . . .

CUT TO:

31. EXT. FIRST AVENUE – NIGHT

6–2 Young heading up the Avenue.

> MARCUS
>
> I ever tell you about the time years ago I was on this ledge uptown, trying to talk this psycho inside?

> FRANK
>
> Where the guy jumped and you almost fell. No, you never told me that story.

> MARCUS
>
> No, you never listened. I was going, man, if someone on high hadn't pulled me in. I had put all I had into saving this dumb-ass lowlife suicidal that when he went down, there was a part of me that wanted to go with him.

> FRANK
>
> Make a left here. I want to stop.

> MARCUS
>
> My point is, everyone has a stretch where folks die on you. Just don't meditate on it.

CUT TO:

32. EXT. BURKE APARTMENT BUILDING – NIGHT

Marcus stops the ambulance on 49th Street.

> FRANK
>
> I'll be right back.

Frank gets out, walks over to the intercom, pushes the button for 5A. Mary answers:

                        MARY
                       (O.S.)
Yes?

                        FRANK
Hello, it's Frank Pierce, from the ambulance last night. I
brought your father in to the hospital and I just learned some
news.

                        MARY
                       (O.S.)
I'll be right down.

*Frank looks off, waiting. Mary appears in a white sweater and simple
gray skirt like schoolgirls wear. The dark make-up is gone.*

She looks happy.

                        MARY
He's better, isn't he?

                        FRANK
Well, the doctor says he's showing some movement. It's still
early, it might mean nothing, but I thought you'd want to
know.

                        MARY
I knew. I sensed it when I heard your voice.

                        FRANK
You look so different.

                        MARY
I know. It's awful, isn't it? Night of the Living Cheerleaders.

                        FRANK
I think it looks good.

                        MARY
I was going nuts in that waiting room so I came back to check
on my mom.

                        FRANK
How is she?

MARY

Sleeping.

FRANK

I was just going to get some food. Pizza. Maybe we could . . .

MARY

You can't kill my father that easy. He'll fight for ever. Like with me: hasn't talked to me in three years. But it's OK. Sometimes you have to put things behind you.

Mary steps to the curb, raises her hand for a taxi. None in sight.

MARY

I've got to get back.

FRANK

Be tough to get a taxi here. We can give you a ride if you like.

MARY
(*looks at him*)

Okay.

Frank opens the back doors of the bus, climbs in behind Mary. They sit on the bench opposite the stretcher.

MARCUS

Who's that?

FRANK

She's the daughter of a cardiac arrest I brought in last night. I told her we'd give her a ride back to Misery. Her father's showing signs of improving.

MARCUS

Oh, Frank, you've got it bad, so much worse than I thought.

FRANK

I'm hungry too. We gotta get some food after this.

MARCUS

God help us, he's hungry too.

Marcus turns on the radio, an old song from the sixties, as they head uptown.

CUT TO:

33. INT. MERCY CRITICAL CARE – NIGHT

Frank and Mary walking past the triage station towards the curtained corner where her father lies. Next to Burke, Dr Hazmat assists an AIDS patient amid a forest of IV tubing.

Mr Burke lies prone, two IV lines hung from poles, intubated by a hose running to the ventilator, an NG tube covering his nose.

His eyes are permanently half open. Burke's hands and feet are tied by white nylon restraints. Mary takes her father's hand as Frank pulls the curtain.

MARY

Dad, can you hear me?
(beat)
Open your eyes if you can hear me.

A nearby patient screams. Mary Burke screams too:

He squeezed my hand!

Dr Hazmat and Milagros, a nurse, walk over.

MARY

He's moving, Doctor. He grabbed my hand. Move your hand, Dad, one more time.
(Burke's hand twitches)
See. See.

HAZMAT

I'll be damned.
(checks Burke's pupils)
It's movement, but I'm not sure how voluntary.

MARY

He hears me. Open your eyes, Dad.

Burke's eyes, never fully closed, open, shift from his daughter to the side. His cheeks ripple and his lips smack against the tube between them. His back arches, his body shakes, his arms yank at the restraints as if reaching to pull out the wires and tubes. Green lights dance across the EKG screen, alarms sound: first the cardiac monitor, next the ventilator.

HAZMAT

Nurse Crupp, I need ten milligrams of Valium.

Hazmat and Milagros hold down Burke's arms as Crupp prepares the Valium. Mary backs away.

FRANK

Why don't we go outside for a little while, wait until this passes.

They step away.

CUT TO:

34. INT. LOCKER ROOM – NIGHT

Passing Griss (reading anti-white agitprop) and waiting-room regulars, Frank leads Mary to a small rectangular paramedic locker area: sofa, desk, two banks of gray lockers, walls decorated with hospital rules and regulations.

FRANK

He wants to pull that tube out. It's pretty painful – that's why they keep him sedated – but it's a good sign.

MARY

You sure? I know my father would hate to be tied down. He wouldn't even go to the dentist.

He sits across from her, wishing he could be in three seats at once, each to watch her from a different angle.

FRANK

That's how it's done. You have to keep the body going until the brain and heart recover enough to go on their own.

MARY

He's better, though, right?

51

FRANK
(*reluctant*)

He's better.

MARY

Look, I'm sorry, but it's important to me. I mean, a week ago
I was wishing he was dead. And now I want to hear his voice
again, just once more – you know what I mean?

Marcus enters with a small pizza and two Cokes.

MARCUS

Went over to Ray's, got this. There must be some place in
hell for a guy who sells a dollar-fifty a slice. I'll call you if
anything comes up.

FRANK

Thanks.

Marcus exits.

MARY

I'm not really hungry.

She says as she picks up a slice of cheese pizza.

My father was a great man, you know. There was nobody he
wouldn't help. You know that crazy guy Noel who I gave
water to last night? He lived in our house for almost a year. A
total stranger he'd do anything for, his own family though ...

FRANK

It's best not to ...
(*off her look*)

It's good pizza, huh?

MARY

Not as good as Nino's.

FRANK

You remember that pizza place, Mimi's, on Tenth Street
maybe fifteen years ago? When you ordered a pie it came with
a little plastic Madonna in the middle?

MARY

Yeah, or Saint Anthony. You from the neighborhood?

FRANK

I grew up on 43rd. I went to Holy Cross.

MARY

Oh yeah? I went to Sacred Heart. Where'd you go to high school?

FRANK

We moved out after that. Upstate.

MARY

Like everybody else – except us. Always standing on the sidewalk waving goodbye to moving trucks. Your parents . . . ?

FRANK

They're fine. My old man was a bus driver, mom a nurse – I was sort of born to it, I guess.

MARY

You married?

FRANK

Ah, no. I was.
>   (*beat*)
It's hard to explain. She had a hard time adjusting to, well, maybe it was my fault too.

Pause. The thought hangs in the air. From outside: a bellicose drunk is escorted into the ER:

DRUNK
>   (*O.S.*)
White cocksuckers! Get your – OW!

MARY

Is it always this bad in here? I mean, how does anyone survive?

FRANK

It's been bad lately, but it's always bad.

MARY

How long you been doing this?

FRANK

Five years.

MARY

Wow, you musta seen some things, huh? What's the worst
thing you ever seen?

FRANK

You learn to sort of block it out, you know, like cops fence off
a crime scene. But then something good will happen and
everything will just glow.

MARY

You must get a lot of overdoses. I bet you picked me up a
couple of times.

FRANK

I think I'd remember that.

MARY

Maybe not. I was a different person then. Does everybody
you meet spill their problems on you like this?

FRANK

Mostly. It must be my face. My mother always said I looked
like a priest.

MARY

Tell me about it. My mother thought I was gonna be a nun
because I ran away to a convent when I was thirteen. I didn't
want to be a nun. I just wanted to run away. Sister Mary or
Mary the Junkie. Didn't matter to me.
(*wiping mouth*)
I better go check on my father. Thanks for the pizza. I owe
you one. Maybe when he gets better, you know, when we're
done with all this.

FRANK

Sure.

Frank puts his hand out but she's already on her feet. He grabs the last slice of pizza, hands it to Griss as she heads back to Critical Care.

FRANK

> Look after her, Griss, OK?

Griss nods.

CUT TO:

35. EXT. NEW YORK STREETS — NIGHT

6–2 Young back on the job, moving with traffic.

MARCUS

> Rule number one: Don't get involved with patients. Rule
> number two: Don't get involved with patients' daughters.
> You understand?

FRANK

> What about rule number three: Don't get involved with
> dispatchers named Love.

MARCUS

> You don't know the first thing about rule number three,
> cannot begin to understand the complexities of that rule.
> Come on, let's go look at some hookers. The Kit Kat will be
> letting out.
> > *(relevant to nothing)*
> Don't ever call a junkie whore a crackhead. They get real
> mad.

Marcus swings up the Avenue:

> Look at these women. You can't even tell who's a hooker any
> more. Whatever happened to go-go boots and hot pants?
> They wear anything now, walk outta the house with whatever
> they got on . . .

*Frank watches night tableaux (police cars flashing, lovers kissing,
woman crying hysterically, drunken slugfest) as his mind wanders:*

FRANK
(V.O.)

> The street is so much more unpredictable than the ER and to

prepare for the unexpected I was taught to act without thinking, like an army private who can take apart and reassemble a gun blindfolded ...

"Frank notices another EMS bus: Tom Wolls wheeling a stretcher – Noel, face bloodied, lies restrained as Wolls' partner opens the rear doors.

I realized that my training was useful in less than ten per cent of the calls and saving someone's life was rarer than that. As the years went by I grew to understand that my role was less about saving lives than about bearing witness. I was a grief mop and much of my job was to remove, if even for a short time, the grief starter of the grief product. It was enough that I simply showed up.

Marcus continues as if uninterrupted:

MARCUS

... look at her. Leaves you no idea what's underneath, not even a suggestion. Could be a skeleton for all you know.

Dispatch radio plays under:

DISPATCHER LOVE

Seventy-four Will, 330 West 33rd, the Church of Jesus Son, for demonic possession. Seventy-two Victor, you're going to 8th and 14th. On the corner there is a forty-year-old man hearing celebrity voices. Seventy-six Xray, take it uptown 541 West 54th, for the elderly woman abducted by her cat.

They pass a working girl in a rain slicker who pulls off her hood to look at them: a familiar face. The Rose face.

MARCUS

Nice though, pulling back her hood as we drive by. There's a mystery to it, then she shows you.

FRANK

She's no whore, Marcus.

MARCUS

We're all whores, Frank. You know what I'm talking about, the way she looked at me.

FRANK

She wasn't looking at you, man, she was looking at me.

Frank, looking back at the receding Rose face, *hears her faintly say:*

'ROSE'

Why did you kill me, Frank?

FRANK

I didn't kill you.

Marcus, not hearing 'Rose's' voice, replies:

MARCUS

No, you didn't, Frank, thank you. But there's still a couple of hours left on the shift.

FRANK
(*to Marcus*)

Not you.

MARCUS

Hearing voices, my man? That's not a good sign.

FRANK

I just need a drink.

MARCUS

And what do these voices tell you?

FRANK

They say, 'Kill Marcus', OK? I don't need shock treatment. I'm not sick. I need a drink, that's all.

Dispatcher Love's voice cuts through:

DISPATCHER LOVE

Six–two Young, answer the radio. I have a call for you.

MARCUS

She said to me, I love the way you talk on the radio.

DISPATCHER LOVE

I can't wait all night, Young. I'm holding a priority and if you don't answer I'm going to knock you out of service.

> MARCUS
> (*keys radio*)
> Don't worry, hon. Young is here and he's gonna help out –
> just remember, you owe me.

> DISPATCHER LOVE
> You're going to 370 West 98th Street, seventeen-year-old
> female cardiac arrest, no further information.

> MARCUS
> Ten–four, hon.

Marcus hits the siren.

CUT TO:

36. EXT. WEST 98TH STREET – NIGHT

*Marcus and Frank getting out, looking up at an abandoned building
that could have been condemned the day it was built: half the windows
boarded up, others lightless, empty, except for one yellow bulb in the top
right apartment.*

> MARCUS
> I hate this block. It's all junkies. I ain't goin' in there without
> cops.

> FRANK
> I'm going. It's easier than waiting.

Frank reaches for the drug box, heads inside; Marcus follows:

CUT TO:

37. INT. RUNDOWN TENEMENT STAIRWELL – NIGHT

*Frank and Marcus, strapped with equipment, feeling their way up
dark, broken stairs. Marcus aims his flashlight as Frank calls out
advance notice:*

> FRANK
> EMS, ambulance.

*Crack vials crunch under their feet. Ahead, at the top of the stairs, an
Hispanic teenager, Carlos, holds a candle.*

Frank takes double steps, leaving Marcus huffing:

> MARCUS
>
> You want me to kill myself on these stairs? Is that the way a partner acts, forgets the oldest rule, Rule Number Five, Partner Before Patients? Help me.

Frank reaches an arm back for Marcus.

> CARLOS
>
> Please hurry.

CUT TO:

38. INT. RUNDOWN TENEMENT – NIGHT

Frank and Marcus enter the top floor with Carlos. Individual walls have been wholly or partly torn down, creating a warehouse-like space. Crackheads stare at them, their faces lit by candles and lighters.

Carlos leads them to a corner, his share of the seemingly communal space.

Maria, a 17-year-old Hispanic girl, lies moaning on a discarded sofa covered with stained sheets, a hyperventilating heap of linen. Carlos, holding the candle for light, watches anxiously.

> MARCUS
>
> Look at that, a fat junkie. That's a first.

> FRANK
> (*to Maria*)
>
> What's wrong.

Carlos speaks in broken English.

> CARLOS
>
> No English. She has terrible pain in her belly.

> FRANK
> (*hands on stomach*)
>
> She's pregnant.

> CARLOS
>
> No, no, that's impossible. We are virgins. No sex. No underwear.

FRANK

Are you pregnant? *Estas embarazada?*

Maria shakes her head, looks away.

Can you walk? *Puedes caminar?*

She swings at Frank with an open hand.

CARLOS

She say she in great pain.

FRANK

Thanks for the translation.
                    (*to Maria*)
What's your name? *Nombre?*

MARIA

Maria.

FRANK

Let's have a look.

MARCUS
                    (*to Carlos*)
You know each other a long time?

CARLOS

Two years. Ever since we left island.

MARCUS

This is a personal question, but I have to ask it. In all that time, you never had sex?

CARLOS

Never.

MARCUS

Maybe you had a couple beers one night last summer. You know how it happens.

CARLOS

Never. No cigarettes, no drugs, no beers.

MARCUS

No underwear?

CARLOS

We are virgins.

Frank opens Maria's legs, turns to Marcus:

FRANK

Oh Jesus, we'd better go. Call for backup.

Marcus keys the walkie, requests assistance.

FRANK

It's coming.

Maria looks down.

FRANK
(*to Carlos*)

Hold her down.

MARCUS

What's that, Frank?

FRANK

Three legs.

MARCUS

That's too many.

FRANK

Backup?

MARCUS

They're coming.

CARLOS

Is she dying?

FRANK

She's having a baby. Twins.

CARLOS

Es impossible.

FRANK

You can trust me on this one.

CARLOS

It's a miracle.

Listening to distant EMS sirens growing louder, Frank wraps her up.

FRANK

Help me get her up.

Marcus and Carlos bend down, reach under Maria.

CUT TO:

39. INT. RUNDOWN TENEMENT HALLWAY – NIGHT

Squeezing down the stairwell, Marcus tripping, Frank using the wall to keep his place, they carry Maria through the winding dark.

Maria screams. She's about to deliver. Frank, Marcus and Carlos place her on the landing.

FRANK

You take the first one.

Frank swaddles the first premie; Marcus prepares to receive the second. Outside, EMS sirens come to a screeching stop.

Marcus, wrapping the second premie, says to Frank:

MARCUS

It's a boy, Frank. He looks good. How's yours?

Frank looks at the baby in his arms as footsteps echo up the stairs: it's not the baby's face. It's Rose. The soundtrack cuts off. The Rose face.

CUT TO:

40. INT. MERCY ER – NIGHT

Frank rushing past Nurse Constance, carrying a newborn in thermal wrap, passing Noel restrained on a gurney:

FRANK

She had a pulse.

NURSE CONSTANCE

Code! Code Blue!

Hazmat rushing over:

HAZMAT
Oh, Jesus, put her on the monitor. Where's the pediatric code cart?
(Odette arriving with cart)
Odette, give me that tube. All right, flatline – let's do CPR. Step back, Frank. How many months?

FRANK
Can't tell. It was a breech, twins. The other seems okay. Marcus is taking him and the mother to Maternity.

Across the room an obscenity-spouting female crackhead is being restrained by a patrolman and hospital security – adding to the sense of emergency and chaos. Dr Mishra, 50, Pediatric MD, and nurse squeeze toward the newborn, edging Frank back. Mishra takes an osteocatheter out of the cart, forces it into the now obscured baby as Nurse Constance massages the infant's chest.

CRACKHEAD
I'm a mother! I got a daughter! I got rights!

HAZMAT
(yelling across room)
Give her some Valium. Ten mil, stat.

Mishra, worried, checks with Nurse Constance – they're losing the newborn:

MISHRA
Status.

NURSE CONSTANCE
I think there's a pulse. I think.

Frank looking at the EKG monitor – a green flatline – backs away.

MISHRA
Fuck.

NURSE CONSTANCE
Nothing.

Frank walking away, not looking where he's going, backs into Noel's gurney.

NOEL

Excuse me, sir, excuse me, could I please trouble you for one cup of water. The smallest thing in the world to ask for water. A man is dying and that is me.

Noel, his face battered from his encounter with Wolls, pulls at his restraints, howls:

NOEL

For days I've eaten nothing but sand, O Lord, I waited so long.

Hazmat looks over:

HAZMAT

Christ. Who the hell woke him up?

CUT TO:

41. EXT. ELEVENTH AVENUE – NIGHT

6–2 Young on the road again, sky turning blue.

FRANK

Don't give me that look.

MARCUS

What look?

FRANK

You know what I'm talking about. It's all over your face. That I-just-saved-a-little-baby-boy look.

MARCUS

We just saved a little baby boy. Think of it that way.

FRANK

I don't want to hear about it, OK? That's three jobs for the night. It's over. Three jobs and time for a drink. Six a.m., the cocktail hour. Pass the bottle; I know you're holding.

Marcus reaches under the seat, pulls a pint of vodka, a quart of orange juice and two cups out of an old gym bag, passes them to Frank.

MARCUS

The bar is now open.

Frank mixes a screwdriver for Marcus, straight vodka for himself.

FRANK

I hate vodka.

MARCUS

Please, a little decorum if you will. What I was going to say is that, holding that baby in my arms, I felt like I was twenty-one again. A call like that makes me think of going back to three nights a week, not two, start running again, cut down on the drinking.

FRANK
(*pours drink*)

I'll drink to that.

MARCUS
(*raises the cup*)

Here's to the greatest job in the world.

FRANK
(*knocks vodka back*)

Greatest job in the world.

DISPATCHER LOVE

Six–two Young, I have priorities holding. Pick up the radio.

FRANK

Don't do it, Marcus. Tell her the bus died, our radio's not working, our backs are out. Tell her we're too drunk to take any more calls.

MARCUS

Let's do it!
(*keys mike*)

It's Marcus, Love, only for you.

DISPATCHER LOVE

Male diff breather, approximately thirty, West End and 72nd.

MARCUS

Ten–four.

Marcus hits the sirens and lights, accelerates to full speed. The vodka spills; Frank grabs the dash.

MARCUS

I'm coming, Love! I'm coming!

Marcus swings the bus wildly to avoid a cab, skids into a turn – and smack towards a parked truck. Frank covers his face and screams.

CRASH! The ambulance careens off the parked truck, its windows shattering, skids on two wheels, flips on its side. There it sits, wailing, wheels spinning, an upended, helpless turtle.

MARCUS

Shit.

Frank, pulling himself up, looks around, realizes no one is hurt. He climbs out. Marcus cuts off the siren:

MARCUS

Where you going?

FRANK

I quit! I'm through!

MARCUS

Just 'cause you quit, you think the ghosts will quit too? It don't work that way. You got to keep moving, Frank!

Frank walks up Eleventh Avenue, leaving Marcus and the disabled vehicle. The first rays of sun strike the buildings ahead.

CUT TO:

42. EXT. MERCY EMERGENCY – DAYBREAK

Frank turning the corner, checking his watch, about to enter the Dark Bar across the street from the hospital, watching Noel run past him and away, skipping from one foot to the other.

FRANK

So long, Noel.

The Emergency doors open: Mary Burke, head down, looking in neither direction, walks away from Frank. Griss steps out after her. Frank joins him:

FRANK

What's going on, Griss?

GRISS

Your friend there just untied the water beggar. Griss was coming out to thank her. Probably saved Griss a murder charge.
>（*about Mary*）
>Having a tough time of it.

Mary starts to run. Frank follows her through the streets.

She pushes her way through a group of junior high-schoolers; Frank does likewise, keeping his distance.

Frank looks at the laughing girls in their matching uniforms and backpacks: they seem like visitors from another planet.

Five blocks later, Mary hesitates at a plaza outside a West Side Project.

CUT TO:

43. EXT. PROJECTS – MORNING

Frank stops a few steps away from Mary; Mary turns.

FRANK

Excuse me. You seemed like you were in trouble.

MARY
(*steps over*)
I'm all right. I just can't stand to see people tied up. I'm in the waiting room for hours, listening to Noel screaming. The only reason he's screaming is 'cause he's tied up.

FRANK

Don't seem so bad to me.

MARY

Don't say that. I wanted to cut my father loose too. They told me he almost died and five minutes later they say he's better

67

and I go in. It's killing me seeing him fighting like that.
(*gazes up building*)
Look, since you're here, maybe you could do me a favor. I
need you to wait for me outside this building, OK? I have to
visit a friend who's sick.

FRANK

OK.

Mary takes a few steps, turns back.

MARY

I'm only asking because it's a dangerous building. There's
been some robberies, a woman was raped not long ago. This
woman I'm seeing, she'll want to talk to me all day, but if I
can point to you out the window and say you're waiting, I can
be out quick. If anything happens, I'll be in apartment 16M.

FRANK

Maybe I should come up with you.

MARY

If I'm not back in fifteen minutes, hit the buzzer. That way
she'll let me go.

FRANK

Nothing's going to happen. I'll come with you.

MARY

No, I'll be fine. I'm just visiting a sick friend.

She walks into the building. He follows.

CUT TO:

44. INT. ELEVATOR – DAY

*The hinged metal doors shudder shut as Frank follows Mary into the
graffitied elevator. It jumps three feet upwards, stops, then continues,
metal scraping concrete at each passing floor.*

MARY

I shouldn't have asked you to come.

                         FRANK
You asked me not to come.

                         MARY
Promise you won't go inside.

                         FRANK
Fifteen minutes.

                         MARY
Everyone in that hospital is crazy. I'm going crazy too. You
understand. I just have to relax a little. Not feel so guilty.

                         FRANK
We can still go back. I'll walk you home. You sleep a couple
of hours, watch some TV, take a bath.

                         MARY
Don't be a cop.

                         FRANK
If you have any doubts about this, it's my fault.

The elevator jerks to a stop; the doors open.

                                                    CUT TO:

45. INT. SIXTEENTH FLOOR – MORNING

Mary turns to Frank:

                         MARY
You go on home, okay. I'm fine, really. I don't need you.
Thanks.

*Mary pushes the bell at 16M. Kanita, 25, wearing a paisley robe, opens
the doors and says:*

                         KANITA
Hey, Cy, guess who's here?

                         COATES
                         (O.S.)
Mary . . .

The elevator doors close on Frank.

46. INT. LOBBY – MORNING

Frank paces past the sleeping security guard, checks his watch.

He presses the elevator button.

CUT TO:

47. INT. THE OASIS – MORNING

The door to 16M opens:

KANITA

Can I help you?

FRANK

Mary Burke. She's a friend.

KANITA

She's not here.

Frank pushes past her.

KANITA

Wait a minute. You can't go in.

Cy Coates, 45, light-skinned black, stands in the smoky room. Dark-curtained windows block the sunlight; a dirty fish tank casts a green glow across the beat-up furniture. A large framed 3D photo of a volcano hangs over the couch, wisps of smoke puffing from the cone.

COATES

It's okay, Kanita. Come on in.

KANITA

He looks like a cop.

COATES

He's not a cop. He's a medic.
                    (*extends hand*)
I'm Cy Coates.

FRANK

Frank Pierce.

70

COATES

Mary said you might be coming.

FRANK

Where is she?

COATES

Sleeping in the back.

FRANK

She asked me to pick her up. Go out for a movie and a malt, then bring her right home.

COATES

I know, but she told me to tell you she wants to crash here a few hours. Terrible about her father, isn't it?

FRANK

I better just go in and see her.

Kanita sits on the sofa next to an unshaven sleeping man. Coates gestures:

COATES

I call this the Oasis. Refuge from the world out there. Did you know two people were shot in this building last week?

Frank heads down the hall towards the rear of the apartment; Coates follows. They pass an open door where inside Tiger, a fat man with dried blood running down the corner of his mouth, sits punching computer keys at a desk.

Careful. That's the Tiger. The lady's down the hall. Welcome to Dayrise Enterprises, Frank, the stress-free factory.

In the next room Mary lies on a mattress on the floor, yellow sheet pulled up to her neck. Frank leans over her:

FRANK

Mary. Mary, we've got to get going.

MARY
(*groggy*)

No, no.

71

She wanted something to help her sleep.

FRANK

Mary, we really have to go.

Mary blindly swings her fist at him, collapses unconscious back to the mattress.

COATES

Frank, she's suffered enough. She's OK, I promise.
(*puts hand on Frank's shoulder*)
C'mon, Frank.

Coates escorts Frank back to the living-room.

I'm always interested in people in stressful occupations and being a paramedic is about as stressful as I can imagine. Here, sit down. What's it like? Tell me some war stories.

FRANK
(*sits*)

Got a beer?

Coates sits across from him, pulls out a pin-sized joint, lights it:

COATES

That shit is poison, Frank. We don't drink alcohol here. What you need is one of these.

FRANK

Did you give Mary something called Red Death?

COATES

Red Death?
(*passes joint to Kanita*)
Tell me something, Frank – does killing your clients make good business sense to you? The kids selling that shit have no sense. They'll be taken care of, don't worry about that.

FRANK

I should be going. I just quit.

COATES

Sleep is all stress reduction. Here.

(offers white pill)
You take one of these, sleep two hours, that's all you need.
(Frank hesitates)
Why do you think I'm telling you this – for *my* health? You ought to look at yourself in the mirror, man. Kanita, get him a glass of water.

Frank watches as Kanita gets up, walks to the kitchen. Coates places the pill in his hand.

FRANK

Is this what you gave Mary?

COATES

That's the stuff. I call it the Red Lion. Very king-of-the-jungle. No language, only brute power. You can't believe how relaxing it is.

Kanita returns with a glass of water, gives it to Frank; Coates stands, feeds the fish.

COATES

Frank, I'm trying to help you. Drink up.

Frank swallows the white pill, drinks the water. He places his arms on the chair:

FRANK

I guess I'll be going.

COATES

Just take it easy.

Frank looks around the smoke-filled room. Kanita walks over, extends her hand.

KANITA

Take my pulse.
(he does)
It's good, isn't it?

FRANK

Perfect. Three hundred beats per minute.

I knew it. I was wrong about you. You're not so bad.

Kanita runs her hands across his shoulders. Frank starts to nod. The room is getting warm and dark. His eyelids lower: sleep, precious sleep.

CUT TO:

48. FRANK'S ROSE VISION

Voices and sounds echo through the purple haze as Frank's mind drifts in time and space. Action and sounds slow, speed up, distort – intermix with the Oasis – as Frank goes back:

This is how it begins: the last time, the first time...

Larry exits 63 Zebra as Rose, 18, wearing a yellow rain slicker, falls to her knees in the miasmic dream stank, on to the sidewalk, then on to her back. From 40 feet away Frank, seeing her reach for a parking meter, grabbing the tube kit, running.

Rose gasping for breath, Frank falling to his knees, lifting her tongue, prying her teeth apart, slipping the blade between her lips – Rose not breathing: waiting for her to inhale, shooting the tube down her vocal chords. Larry listening to lung sounds, belly sounds:

LARRY

You're in the stomach!

FRANK

You sure?

ROSE

Rose!

FRANK

Huh?

ROSE

My name. Rose.

LARRY

You're in the stomach, man.

Frank pulling the tube out, trying again.

Somewhere: Cy Coates laughs.

> LARRY

You're in the stomach! Let me try.

> FRANK

One more time!

Rose going blue, pulse rate dropping, EKG slowing: Jim Morrison singing.

> LARRY

Stomach again.

> FRANK

No way!

Larry ripping the tube from Frank's hands, taking over, pushing Frank aside, trying CPR, intubating Rose, air moving into her lungs – it doesn't matter. Rose is fading.

And as she does: flying into frame to replace her, like some manic jack-in-the-box jokester, is Noel's Face, *cackling.*

Frank hears a scream: it's his own voice.

CUT TO:

49. INT. THE OASIS – DAY

Frank standing screaming in the living-room. Coates walking over, Kanita standing, the sleeping man waking.

> COATES

Frank, take it easy. What happened?

> KANITA

He flipped out.

Frank bends over in pain.

> COATES

Be cool, man. You're having a paradoxical reaction. It can happen.
> (*to Kanita*)
Didn't I tell you this guy was stressed out?

KANITA

Stressed? He's psycho.

Frank heads to where Mary sleeps.

COATES

Frank, where you going?

In the back bedroom, Frank picks up Mary, hoists her over his shoulder fireman-style and heads out. Tiger comes out, stands by Coates.

COATES

You're making a mistake. Sit down and relax a minute.

Frank opens the front door – no one stops him – exits.

COATES
(*calling*)

She'll be back. And, by the way, you owe me ten bucks!

CUT TO:

50. INT. PROJECT LOBBY – DAY

The elevator doors open. Frank sets Mary on her feet.

MARY

I can walk.

She says, weaving out of the front doors.

CUT TO:

51. EXT. PROJECT – DAY

Mary walks a few steps into the plaza, stumbles; Frank catches her.

MARY

Let go of me.
(*he relaxes*)
You shouldn't have come up. I told you not to. You could have gotten us both killed.

Mary heads up the avenue: past baby strollers, postal workers, deliverymen. Visitors from the Planet Daytime.

MARY

You and Cy have a nice talk? He tell you about Dayrise Enterprises, helping people? Well, I've seen him hurt people. Why are you following me?

FRANK

Because you can barely walk.

Frank, walking slightly beside and behind, lights a cigarette.

MARY

You remember Noel, from the other night, how Noel is now? He was my brother's best friend. Cy or Tiger or one of those other goons put a bullet in Noel's head. He was in a coma three months. Crazy ever since.

They stop at a three-story brick apartment building.

This is my place.

She unlocks the door. He follow her in.

CUT TO:

52. INT. MARY'S APARTMENT BUILDING – DAY

Mary grabs the railing, heads up the stairs.

MARY

What is it? You want to help me, you feel sorry for me? Keep it to yourself.

FRANK

I need to sit down a minute.

MARY

You wanna fuck me? Everyone else has.

Mary opens the door to her first-floor apartment; Frank follows. The room is clean and feminine. Unframed water-colors stacked against the wall atop a desk. A black Lab greets Mary, she pets him. Frank slumps on the sofa.

MARY

I've been clean two years now. I got a job. I paint when I'm home. Don't bother anybody. Then all this shit happens.

Frank keels over on to his side, his head hitting a cushion, eyes closed, dog licking his cheek.

> MARY

Oh no you don't. You can't stay here.

He's asleep, the sound of her crying fading in his head.

CUT TO:

53. INT. MARY'S APARTMENT – NIGHT

FADE IN: *a passing siren wakes Frank. He thinks back, looking around the darkened room, realizes where he is. The dog comes over, licks his hand.*

> FRANK

Hello, I'm Frank. Mary's friend. A very close friend who loves animals.

He removes the blanket Mary has laid over him, stands:

Hello?

Frank walks cautiously through the dark, finds a bathroom lit by a glowing Mickey Mouse switch. He flips on the switch: a string of green and red Christmas lights glow. Three types of soap sit on the sink. He turns on the faucet:

> FRANK
> (*V.O.*)

I washed my face with three kinds of soap, each smelling like a different season. It felt good to be in a woman's room again, especially a woman who wasn't comatose or severely disabled. I felt like perhaps I had turned a corner, like I saved someone, though I didn't know who.

CUT TO:

54. INT. EMS GARAGE – NIGHT

Frank standing at Captain Barney's desk.

> CAPTAIN BARNEY

You're late, Pierce. I know, but I can't fire you. I've got nobody to work Sixty-six Xray with Wolls.

FRANK

No ...

CAPTAIN BARNEY

I got some forms here to fill out about that accident when you got the time.

(*hands him keys*)

I'll fire you tomorrow. I promise.

FRANK

What if there is no tomorrow?

CAPTAIN BARNEY

Go on, get outta here, Pierce, before I gave you a big hug.

(*to Miss Williams*)

I love this guy.

CUT TO:

55. EXT. MERCY EMERGENCY – NIGHT

Frank walks toward 66 Xray as Wolls gets out of the front seat.

The EMS vehicle is a relic of wars: the sides and front chewed with dents, a municipal-brown rust spread like a rash from the hood to the pitted lower panels.

Wolls punches Frank joyously:

WOLLS

Frank, what do you know? It's you and me again tonight, the Rough Riders, tearing up the streets just like old times.

(*kicks the front tire*)

This old bus is a warrior, Frank, just like us. I have tried to kill him and he will not die. I have a great respect for that.

Frank makes a 'be right back' gesture, walks into the ER.

CUT TO:

56. INT. MERCY ER – NIGHT

Saturday night at the Knife and Gun Club: the joint is hopping, the sound system blaring.

Frank passing Griss, holding back an angry Hispanic man with a bleeding arm:

GRISS

Don't make me take off my sunglasses.

FRANK

Morning, Griss.

GRISS

We're full up tonight, Frank.

Frank walks over to unit three, Mr Burke's cubicle, pulls back the curtain. Burke lies sedated, wired and tubed. Frank leans over, feels Burke's pulse.

Frank's expression changes – he looks at the EKG monitor: green lines seem to be at war, normal beats marching in formation against wild-looking rhythms, the heart working hard and not getting much done.

Burke's face twitches. Burke's voice speaks in Frank's head:

BURKE'S VOICE

Go to the bank, boy, take out everything you can.

Frank turns up the EKG amplitude.

FRANK

Mr Burke?

BURKE'S VOICE

I'm going. I've had enough.

The alarms start to ring: EKG first, followed by the bells of the oxygen saturation monitor and low drone of the ventilator.

Nurse Milagros pulling open the curtain behind Frank, shaking her head, reaching for the defibrillator paddles, handing them to Frank. He steps back:

FRANK

You do it.

MILAGROS

Can't reach. You're taller.

BURKE'S VOICE

Don't do it.

FRANK

I though he was getting better.

MILAGROS

Better than what?

FRANK

But . . .

MILAGROS

It doesn't matter.

FRANK

Why not?

MILAGROS

The family wants us to keep him alive, so that's that. The wife wants to believe in miracles, we keep him alive. Shock him, Frank. He'll come back. He always comes back.

FRANK
(*takes paddles*)

Clear!

Frank, leaning over, shocks Burke.

BURKE'S VOICE

You son of a bitch.

MILAGROS
(*looking at Burke's monitor*)

Shock him again.

Burke's vacant eyes plead: no. Frank, reluctant, positions the paddles. One of the paddles touches his shoulder by mistake: Frank jerks involuntarily back as if hit with a cattle prod.

MILAGROS

Jesus.

NURSE CRUPP
(*stopping*)

You OK?

Milagros, watching the monitor, takes the paddles from Frank, shocks Burke again.

BURKE'S VOICE

Ow!

Burke's heartbeats resume a regular formation. Frank, despondent, working his sore shoulder, walks away.

BURKE'S VOICE

Hey, boy! Where are you going, Frank?

WOLLS

Come on, Frank. There's blood spilling in the streets.

Frank crawls back in front carrying the IV bag, puts on the oxygen mask, turns on the main tanks, takes a deep hit.

FRANK
(*pulls off mask*)

These are hard times, Tom.

WOLLS

Yeah. Great, isn't it?

FRANK

Great to be drunk. Sobriety's killing me.

WOLLS

Look up, Frank. Full moon. The blood's gonna run tonight. I can feel it. Our mission: to save lives.

FRANK

Our mission is coffee, Tom. A shot of the bull, Puerto Rican espresso.

WOLLS

Ten–four. El Toro de Oro. Blast off.

Wolls hits the sirens, accelerates.

FRANK

The cure's not working, Tom. Maybe we should go back to the hospital.

WOLLS

Don't worry, kid. Tom'll take care of you. Put your head out the window, get some of that summer air. Listen to the music. El Toro de Oro. Andale. Pronto.

Wolls turns up the radio, drums his hands against the wheel.

DISPATCHER

OK, units, it's suicide hour. Seventy-four Boy, I show you in the hospital sixty minutes but I know you're in the diner on 14th. Put down the burger, I got a call for you around the corner, 14 and 7th, a man with a noose around his neck and nothing to hang it on. Sixty-six Xray, don't even think about getting coffee, I have a call for you too.

WOLLS
(*on radio*)

Six–six Xterminator here. We like our coffee bloody. Make it good – my partner's dying to help someone.

DISPATCHER

You're in luck, X: your patient awaits you with bleeding wrists in the homeless tunnel.

Frank pulls the IV needle out of his arm, searches the glove compartment.

FRANK

Tom, where are the Band-Aids? This is an ambulance, isn't it?

WOLLS
(*hitting the gas*)

Look out!

66 Xray lurches forward.

CUT TO:

83

66 Xray breaks to a stop before a two-dozen-strong cluster of derelicts, junkies and night people. Frank and Tom look around, trying to guess which patient is theirs. Two drunks are trying to help a friend with cut wrists.

> WOLLS

What the hell's going on?

> DRUNK #1

You've gotta take him to the hospital. He tried to kill himself. Show him your wrist. Show it.

Cut Wrists gets up, leans against the ambulance, shaking.

> DRUNK #1

See, he ain't right.

> WOLLS

Hold it. I will not take anyone anywhere against his will. This is America. People have rights.

> DRUNK #2

He was bleeding before. He kept spilling his beer. I gave him mouth-to-mouth.

> WOLLS

You're lucky you didn't kill him.
> (*to Cut Wrists*)
We're going to hear it straight from the loony's mouth. Are you crazy? Did you try to bump yourself off?

> CUT WRISTS
> (*salivatory*)

Yesssss.

> WOLLS

Why didn't you say so?

Wolls escorts Cut Wrists into the back of the bus, pulls a plastic electric patch off the EKG monitor. Frank joins them.

> WOLLS

Sir, I am going to give you some medicine that is still very

experimental. It's from NASA and although the astronauts
have been using it for years, we are the first service to try it. I
will put this patch on your forehead like this, and in about a
minute you will have to relax.

(*places patch*)

You will forget all your suicidal feelings. It's very important
that you wear this for at least twenty-four hours and keep
checking the mirror. If the patch turns green you have to see a
doctor immediately. The side effects could be fatal.

Cut Wrists nods.

FRANK

This is the worst suicide attempt I've ever seen. You feel that
pulse? Here. That's where you cut, and it's not across, it's
down like so.

(*takes out his knife*)

Here, take it.

CUT WRISTS
(*shaking*)

I can't.

FRANK

With all the poor people of this city who wanted only to live
and were viciously murdered, you have the nerve to sit here
waiting to die and not go through with it. You make me sick.
Take it.

*Cut Wrists bolts out of the back of the bus, trips as he hits the road, runs
down the street, turning the corner still holding the patch to his forehead.*

WOLLS

We cured him, Frank. When we work together there's
nothing we can't fix.

CUT TO:

59. EXT. EL TORO DE ORO – NIGHT

66 Xray parked outside a fluorescent chrome and plastic coffee shop.

CUT TO:

60. INT. EL TORO DE ORO – NIGHT

A young downtowner shouts into a phone mounted on the wall:

> DOWNTOWNER
>
> Don't lie to me I know where you been I called you your brother says you been out all day don't lie to me I'll kill you bitch.

Slamming the phone down, he punches the wall, throws himself into a chair next to his two friends, laughing.

Frank, watching, smoking at a formica table, his walkie-talkie upright next to an ashtray. Wolls returns with two espressos as the dispatcher rattles on.

> WOLLS
> (*sits*)
>
> Sounds like they're trying to clean up the bus terminal tonight.

Frank doesn't answer. Tom shines his mini-flashlight in Frank's eyes:

> Hello, hello. Major Tom to Frank, time to come home.

Frank watches a hooker on the sidewalk. Two street punks dripping gold and attitude head the opposite direction: one turns his head, looks at Frank – it's Rose. The Rose face.

Frank getting up, grabbing his walkie and coffee, heading out.

> WOLLS
>
> Where you going?

> FRANK
>
> C'mon, Tom. The city's burning.

CUT TO:

61. EXT. NEW YORK STREET – NIGHT

Frank at the wheel, driving fast, radio blasting INXS's 'Devil Inside'. Frank's POV: the streets.

> WOLLS
>
> Whatja doing?

FRANK

I feel the need, the need for speed. I'm driving out of myself.

WOLLS

The brakes are shot.

FRANK

I've taken that into consideration.

WOLLS

You OK?

FRANK

I never felt better in my life.

DISPATCHER

Sixty-six Xray, Xray.

FRANK
(*keys radio*)

X.

DISPATCHER

First of all, I want you to know how sorry I am about this. I've always liked you two. A unit above none, a legend in its own lunchtime, so it hurts me deeply to do this but I have no choice. You must go to 48th and Broadway. In front of a liquor store you'll find a forty-year-old male, unconscious, lying next to his wheelchair. Do I have to say more?

FRANK
(*to radio*)

You've said too much already.

WOLLS

Mr Oh.

FRANK

It's early for him.

WOLLS

That's all right, we're not meant to do Oh tonight. Something is going to happen. I can feel it.

Tom hears something on the police radio: a call for units to The Projects.

Bingo.
                    (*keys police walkie*)
EMS to Central. What was that call?

                    POLICE DISPATCH
A jumper. West Side Projects.

                    WOLLS
Ten–four. One minute out.

                    DISPATCHER
                    (*urgent*)
Sixty-six, Sixty-six Xray. Level One Emergency.

But they're not listening – Frank's off to The Projects.

The Dispatcher, maxed out, hysterical, spits out words as the tires squeal:

                    DISPATCHER
I need units. I need units. We got fires in the hole, Eighth and
Broadway. Shots fired outside the Dynamite Club, 13th and
6th. Fired workers shooting each other at the post office.
Where are my units?

                                        CUT TO:

62. EXT. PROJECTS – NIGHT

*Police cars, fire engines, a massive Emergency Service rescue truck all
flashing dome lights on the street, on the plaza surrounding Cy Coates'
building: cops, SWAT team, spotlights, onlookers.*

*Frank and Tom, getting out, looking up: the spotlit figure of Cy Coates,
13 floors above, suspended on a railing, legs dangling.*

*Two men incongruously dressed like rabbis aim the spotlight fixed on
Coates. Tom turns to a fireman:*

                    WOLLS
What's with the rabbis?

                    FIREMAN
They like to follow us around. We deputized 'em. They put
up the money for a new truck.

Frank hears a familiar voice: Sister Fetus has made the scene. She stands outside a deli lecturing passersby:

SISTER FETUS

... as John foretold, fire will be the sky, fire the ocean and the fields, everlasting fire the air you breathe everlastingly.
(*to inattentive onlookers*)
Go on home, sinners, ignore the last call. Go back to your opium pipes and whiskey bottles, back to your child pornography and gay marriages. Back to your slot machines, ribbed condoms, Mexican divorces, your sex clubs and martinis. Back to your hot-oil wrestling, Washington lobbying, organ donation. The list is long but it's all written down – your state-subsidized brothels, liposuction, Oriental cooking. Add it up, you know what it spells. F–I–R–E.

Wolls turns to Frank:

WOLLS

Whadda we bring?

FRANK

Better bring it all.

CUT TO:

63. INT. LOBBY – NIGHT

Frank and Tom, lugging their equipment, meet up with cops, firemen and their rescue equipment.

FRANK

The elevator's fucked. We'd never fit anyway. Let's go.

FIREMAN

That's thirteen flights.

WOLLS

The news guys just pulled up.

POLICE SERGEANT

The stairs, men, the stairs.

The sergeant leads a half-dozen cops and firemen up the stairs as the elevator doors open. Tom, Frank and two cops squeeze inside.

WOLLS

This guy a jumper?

ELEVATOR COP #1

We got a call for shots fired on the sixteenth floor. The jumper called right after.

FRANK
(to Wolls)

I'm going to sixteen.

As the elevator doors close.

CUT TO:

64. INT. THE OASIS – NIGHT

Frank exiting the elevator with the officers. Their feet slosh on the water-soaked carpet.

The door to 16M is open: Kanita lies half-in, half-out the door, a perfectly round hole above her eye, splinters of bone and blood down the side of her nose.

ELEVATOR COP #1
(stepping over Kanita)

She must have left the tub on.

The carpet is soaked with water; shards of glass lie amid dying fish. A cop returns from the rear hall of the apartment, stands before the puffing photo of volcano:

ELEVATOR COP #2

That's it, nobody else home.

Frank, looking over the balcony, sees Coates three floors below.

FRANK

I'm going to thirteen.

Frank heads down the stairs.

CUT TO:

65. INT. THIRTEENTH FLOOR – NIGHT

Frank emerges on thirteen, enters 13m.

Wolls, the panting police sergeant and team have overturned the furniture: the absent owners would have trouble recognizing it. The floor is covered with gas-powered metal cutters, acetylene torches, ropes, harnesses.

The balcony door windows are broken; sound of voices comes from outside. Frank steps over to Wolls.

WOLLS
Get this, Frank – we got two patients. Number one, the scarecrow outside. Number two, the big fella, misses the railing but breaks both legs on the balcony, then throws himself through a glass window, heads to the bedroom, where he's now passed out.

Wolls motions to a trail of blood leading to the bedroom where Tiger lies on the carpet, passed out and handcuffed. Frank looks on to the balcony where Coates hangs:

FRANK
Well, he's the steakhead of the night, then.

WOLLS
I don't think the fire people can touch him out there.

FRANK
How's he doing?

WOLLS
I haven't had a chance to see him yet. I'm going to take care of sleeping beauty.

Frank goes over to Coates as two cops strap on harnesses. Coates hangs impaled on the railing, a steel spike passing through his hip.

Glowing in spotlights from thirteen floors below, Frank takes Coates's vital signs, gently presses his abdomen:

FRANK
Does that hurt?

COATES
(*screams*)

No!

Frank, IV bag in his teeth, putting an oxygen mask on Coates:

FRANK
I don't think you've hurt any major organs.
(*sets IV line*)
We got to get you off this thing without setting off bleeding.

Cops behind click on harnesses ('You in?' 'Yeah.' 'You in?'), attach straps to pitons they've hammered into the brick wall, bring out metal cutters and torches.

The cop, leaning over, saying so 'maybe' Frank can hear:

COP
He happens to fall, I don't think anybody'll be crying too much.

FRANK
They're gonna torch the fence. You're gonna feel the metal getting warm, maybe very warm.

COATES
I can't hold my head up any more.

Frank passes the IV bag to one of the cops, holds Coates's head. Cy relaxes his neck as sparks splay like fireworks beneath him, fall to the concrete.

So, Frank, am I going to live?

FRANK
You're going to live.

COATES
The ten dollars you owe me?

FRANK
Yeah?

COATES
Keep it. I've been thinking about things. Meditating on my

financial future. You guys gave me plenty of time to meditate on the future. Whatja do, stop for Chinese on the way over? There's plenty of food at my place.

FRANK

I was tired. I needed a coffee.

COATES

What about Kanita?

FRANK

Dead.

COATES

That's too bad. Get some money, a nice-looking girl on your arm, and everyone wants to take a piece. Some kid I wouldn't let wash my Mercedes is in my house, shooting at me. Damn, I thought I could make it on to the balcony like Tiger. He's fat, that's why, falls faster. I'm trying to watch my weight, and look what happens. Am I shot, Frank?

FRANK

No.

COATES

Boy can't shoot for shit, either. Goddamn that's hot.

Frank looks: the spike in Coates's hip starting to glow red. Coates stretches his hand toward the skyline, his face backlit by raining acetylene sparks.

COATES

Isn't it beautiful? When the fires start to fall, then the strongest rule it all. I love this city.

The torch breaks the spike free: Frank and Coates freefall three feet, jerk to a stop. Coates yelps. The crowd cheers from below – a voice yelling, 'Let him go!'

Frank now grabbing, holding Coates tightly – his hands the only thing keeping Coates from falling – as the cops hoist them up.

COP #1
(*to Frank*)
Good thing we buckled you in, huh?

COATES

What about me? Who's supposed to buckle me?

COP #2
(*to first cop*)

I thought you did.

COP #1

I thought *you* did.

COP #2
(*to Coates*)

I'm so sorry, sir.

The cops lift Frank and Coates on to the balcony. One bumps the spike in his hip. He yelps:

COATES

Stop jerking my pole!

CUT TO:

66. EXT. MERCY EMERGENCY – NIGHT

66 *Xray parked in front.*

CUT TO:

67. INT. MERCY CRITICAL CARE – NIGHT

Frank walking out of the restroom wiping water off his face, looking at the gurney where Coates lies on his side, metal spike still sticking through his hip, IV line running to his arm, eyes closed. Nurses walk past Coates: he's stabilized, waiting his turn. Coates take a number.

Frank walks the corridor toward Coates.

COATES

You saved my life, Frank.

FRANK

Then tell me, Cy: why don't I feel good about that?

Frank spots Hazmat at Burke's cubicle, walks over.

HAZMAT

Nurse Crupp, we're going to need some Valium here. He's waking up again.

The ventilator alarm goes off as Burke pulls at his restraints.

HAZMAT
(*urgent*)

Where's the Valium?

Nurse Crupp walks briskly over, injects needle into one of Burke's IV bags.

Burke's voice speaks in Frank's head:

BURKE'S VOICE

Don't. Don't do it.

HAZMAT

Give me a hand, Frank. I've got to get something between those teeth.

Frank helps Hazmat force in a bite stick. The monitor alarm cuts off, the ventilator starts up again, pumping air in, pulling air out.

FRANK

How many times have you shocked him tonight?

HAZMAT

Fourteen. We finally got him a room in the ICU. Should be there in a couple of hours.

FRANK

What will you do, just have someone follow him around with a defibrillator?

HAZMAT
(*laughs*)

That's good, Frank. No, maybe they'll surgically implant one, about the size of my thumb. It goes near the shoulder here, with two electrodes connected to the heart. It sends a shock whenever it senses a drop in blood flow.

MILAGROS

Should I increase the Lidocane?

Frank, not listening, walks away.

68. INT. ER WAITING ROOM – NIGHT

Frank notices Mary Burke in the waiting area with her brother, mother and several others. Gone is the lost daughter, the scared junkie.

Tonight she's dressed for strength: leather jacket, blue jeans, black work boots.

> MARY
>
> Everyone, this is the medic who brought my father in. Frank, these are some of my father's friends.

Frank greets them.

> FAMILY FRIEND
>
> We live out on the Island now, but we used to live right down the block from Pat. He was like a saint to us. Came as soon as we heard.

> FRANK
> (*to Mary*)
>
> I'm going out for a smoke.

Mary whispers something to her mother, joins him.

CUT TO:

69. EXT. MERCY EMERGENCY – NIGHT

Frank offers her a cigarette. Wolls waits in 66 Xray, now parked on the curb.

> MARY
>
> I heard Cy Coates was brought in. He looked pretty bad.

> FRANK
>
> He'll be all right.

> MARY
>
> Too bad. He called me up today, can you believe that? He asks me do I want to come over and see him, I tell him I'd rather go to a leper colony. He says there's a new gang that wants to kill him, take over the business. I told him I hope

he's right. That they kill him. That's what I told him.
>   (*beat*)
Look, last night I was weak. It won't happen again. And all
that shit I said – it was just because I was stoned. Forget it.

>   FRANK
No problem. Thanks for letting me crash. It was the best
sleep I've had in months. I used some of your soap.

>   MARY
I wish these people would leave already. I can't listen to
another story. Did you see him?
>   (*Frank doesn't answer*)
The doctor says the brain is coming around. They're waiting
for the heart to stabilize. I don't know who to believe. He says
they still have to keep him tied up.

>   FRANK
Can I bring you back something to eat – a falafal, some pizza?

>   MARY
No, we just ate. I only remember how tough my father was.
Now I know he had to be like that, to make us tough. This
city'll kill you if you aren't strong enough.

>   FRANK
No, the city doesn't discriminate. It gets everybody.

Wolls flashes 66 Xray's headlights, hits the horn.

> I gotta go. Another call.

Frank, his heart pounding, steps closer to her.

> We're all dying, Mary Burke.

He leans as if to kiss her. She hesitates.

*He places his hand on her shoulder, kisses her cheek lightly, walks
toward Wolls and the waiting ambulance.*

70. EXT. NEW YORK STREETS – NIGHT

*66 Xray is cooking now – Wolls at the wheel, Frank shotgun, drinking
from a pint of whiskey: radio blasting –*

Frank's POV: The streets pulse with high-speed activity. Then with a crunch of gears, transforms into slow motion only to speed up again.

> WOLLS

Get ready, Frank. Missed a drug shooting while you were dicking around in there. There's gonna be trauma tonight!

> FRANK

As long as we keep moving, no standing still.

> WOLLS
> (*keys mike*)

C'mon, look at your screen. Give us some blood!

> DISPATCHER

Sixty-six Xray, a man at the bus terminal shot three years ago says his arm hurts.

Frank looks at a group of girls exiting an after-hours club: every one a Rose. The Rose face.

> FRANK

C'mon Tom. Pick up a job.

> WOLLS

You want some bum in the bus terminal? We'll wait for a real call.

> FRANK

Let's get in a fight, then.

> WOLLS

Who with?

> FRANK

That's your job. Just keep driving, keep moving. No stopping. We're sharks. We stop too long, we die.

Wolls hits the accelerator: the old bus jerks forward:

Let's break something, Tom. Let's bust something, bomb something.

> WOLLS

What do you want to break?

FRANK
(*taking a drink*)
I don't know – let's break some windows.

WOLLS
Why?

FRANK
Destruction, distraction. I feel the need.

WOLLS
You need a reason, Frank. You don't just go around breaking people's windows. That's anarchy.

FRANK
What's the reason? Give me a reason, Tom.

WOLLS
Let me think.

Wolls hits the siren as he swings wildly around a stopped cab and its turban-headed driver:

Classic cabbie move.
(*to driver*)
Hey, Swami, that's called a crosswalk. You stop before it, not on it.

Wolls turns on to a cross street, spots Noel standing by a Mustang, baseball bat on his shoulder. He wears yesterday's bloodstained clothes, cut tires tied to his shoulders and elbows, chest and belly wrapped in steel wire, at least a mile of it, and around his bare brown arms and neck he's tied blue and black rags – rags also around his black boots and rags woven between the thick clumps of black dreadlocks tied wildly with colored string. He wears two watches on each wrist, checking the time on all of them.

I know who to work over. Him.

Wolls slows as Noel lifts the bat, swings it into the Mustang's front window, shattering it, puts the bat down, using it like a cane as he walks to the next parked car.

This guy's been terrorizing the neighborhood for weeks, ever

since he got outta jail, wreaking general havoc, contributing
to the bad name of the place. The term 'menace to society'
was made up for him.

FRANK

He's crazy. He can't help it.

WOLLS
(*stops ambulance*)
Well, why don't they put him away? Prisons don't want him. I
took him to the hospital yesterday and here he is again.

*Noel reaches the next car, a Bronco, carefully hefts the bat, smashes it
through the windshield.*

Look at that. Tell me that's a crazy person. Every move is
calculated. He knows exactly what he's doing. This is the guy.
I've been after him for weeks. He's quick, runs like a rat,
tough for one person, but with two of us –

FRANK

OK, whatta I do?

WOLLS

If he sees me, he'll run, so I'll get out here. You start talking
to him about baseball or something while I sneak around
behind and get down and you push him. When he falls we get
him.

FRANK

That's ridiculous.

WOLLS

Believe me, it always works. The simpler, the better.

FRANK

You learn that in the Army?

WOLLS

Flatbush.

*Wolls slips out, crouches beside the bus. Frank, stepping out, walks over
to Noel as he whacks the bat through the hatch of a Pinto.*

That's a hell of a swing you got there, Noel. I'm thinking
Mattingly in his prime.

NOEL

Mattingly ain't shit.
                    (*heads for the next car*)
Me, I swing like Reggie. Mr October. Number three, game
six, World Series.

*Noel hauls back, lays into a Volvo: glass shatters. Noel holds the bat
out, extends handle toward Frank:*

Here, you try.

FRANK

No, I'd better not.

NOEL

Sure, sure, give it a go.

FRANK

Yeah?

*Frank, intrigued by Noel's suggestion, has forgotten Wolls's plan. He
takes the bat as Wolls sneaks behind Noel, crouching.*

What the hell.
                    (*spits into hands*)
The next year, tie-breaker for the division, in Boston, Yanks
down two to nothing, Bucky Dent steps to the plate.

NOEL

Oh man, lucky fucky Bucky.

FRANK

The pitch, high heater. Bucky knows what's coming. He steps
in, smash, over the green monster.

*Frank cocks the baseball bat, relishing every moment, swings into the
Volvo's side window. Shattered glass flies on his hands and clothes.*

Wolls, fed up with this, stands:

Frank, what the hell are you doing?

Noel, seeing Wolls, grabs the bat, flees down the alley.

You go down those stairs there. Meet me back here if you can't find him in ten minutes. Call out if you see him. Get with the program, Frank.

Wolls takes off after Noel. Frank, taking out his flashlight, enters second alley, walks down dark stairs which hopefully circle around to Noel.

CUT TO:

71. INT. ALLEY – NIGHT

Mini-flashlight leading the way, Frank steps gingerly down the refuse-strewn alley. Ahead: footsteps.

He kicks something, thinking it's trash, looks down: a body rustles, pair of sleeping eyes look up.

Suddenly everything seems silent. He passes a row of glowing red doors. Shadows flash in the distance. He hears a woman crying, shoots the flashlight in her direction: nothing.

Frank hears a voice again: Rose's voice.

'ROSE'

Why did you kill me, Frank?

FRANK

I didn't mean to.

'ROSE'

You should have helped me.

FRANK

I tried to help. I wanted to.

Shadows like hands extend against the wall ahead.

FRANK

Rose?

Don't you love me?

Frank moves toward reaching arms. The shadows swing like baseball bats. Noel screams.

Suddenly, before him, a blurry mass of bloody dreadlocks – Noel goes flying to the ground, Wolls standing over him swinging the bat, hitting him, killing him.

WOLLS

I got him, Frank!

Frank stands back, watching Wolls and Noel like some static black-and-white TV screen from his childhood. Noel, trying to protect himself, cries out.

(*swinging bat*)
To the moon, Alice! You little motherfucker!

Frank charges forward into Wolls, sending him and the baseball bat flying. Wolls on the ground. Frank bends over Noel: Noel's face covered with blood, gasping for air, blowing red bubbles, convulsing.

FRANK
(*to Wolls*)
Get the kit! We're gonna tube him!

WOLLS

Frank!

FRANK

Do it!

WOLLS
(*standing*)

Frank!

FRANK
(*to Noel*)
We're gonna save you, Noel. You're gonna be all right.
(*to Wolls*)
Do it, Tom! I'll call for fucking backup, I swear!

WOLLS

You're crazy.

Noel unconscious: Wolls hurries down the alley toward the ambulance as Frank opens Noel's mouth.

FRANK

You're going to make it! You're going to make it!

Pressing Noel's chest, Frank lowers his mouth, starts CPR. His mouth to Noel's. In the distance: Wolls's footsteps returning.

CUT TO:

73. EXT. MERCY EMERGENCY – NIGHT

66 Xray parked out front; the sky is going blue.

CUT TO:

73. INT. MERCY ER – NIGHT

Frank and Wolls, their shirts bloodstained, pushing Noel down Skid Row, past Griss, past Nurse Constance. Wolls wheels, Frank carries IV bag.

NURSE CONSTANCE

Take him straight through.

GRISS

Who got that funky motherfucker this time?

FRANK
(*to Nurse Constance*)

Last show of the night.

HAZMAT
(*arriving*)

Jesus Christ! Nurse Crupp! Anybody else hurt?

FRANK

No.

Nurse Crupp takes control of the gurney from Wolls who, embarrassed over his role in this whole sad affair, slinks away, heads toward the exit. Frank pushes Noel past Griss holding back waiting for ER patients:

People, hear me out. The path to your well-being and
salvation will not be paved over Griss's body. You can forget
about that, 'cause Griss gets off in forty-seven minutes and
then he's going home to take a bath ...

*Frank accompanied by Milagros and Crupp, wheels Noel into unit one.
Coates sleeps in three, Burke's old unit.*

*Milagros goes to work. Frank brushes the bloody dreadlocks from Noel's
face. Crupp, cutting Noel's clothes, elbows Frank back.*

74. INT. ICU – NIGHT

*Frank Pierce walks down the corridor, steps into ICU room 212, a large
room lined with four beds, each curtained off. An ICU nurse, sitting at
a desk facing four units, writes in her log. The glow of four EKG
monitors reflects off her face and notebook.*

FRANK
Is Patrick Burke here? I brought him in.

*The ICU Nurse points to the fourth stall. Frank steps over to Burke's
bed, closes the curtain behind him.*

*Burke lies, tubed and wired to life support. On the monitor: a slow
steady line, up, down.*

*Burke seems no longer of this world: a captive space alien being kept
alive by government scientists. His half-open eyes fix on Frank. Burke's
voice speaks in Frank's head:*

BURKE'S VOICE
Frank?

FRANK
Yes?

BURKE'S VOICE
Where have you been?

FRANK
What is it?

Let me go.

Frank takes a moment, exhales.

With one hand he unbuttons his shirt. With the other takes three EKG patches from the shelf, attaches them to his chest. He quickly transfers the wires from Burke's patches to his own. Only the slightest variation registers on the monitor.

Frank then transfers the blood pressure cuff from Burke's arm to his, moves the pulse oxymeter from Burke's finger to his own.

Finally, he disconnects the respirator tube from Burke's mouth, places it in his own.

Frank watches Burke, pulls the chair close with his foot. He sits, feels Burke's pulse dropping. Feels the life go out of Burke. Burke shudders, dies.

The ICU Nurse checks her watch, stands to go to the bathroom. A step away from her desk, she hears alarms sound from Burke's unit.

Rushing over, the Nurse pulls back the curtain. There she sees Frank, sweating, trying to revive patient Burke, now wired and tubed as before. Frank, in his haste, has misbuttoned his shirt.

ICU NURSE

Code!

She pushes past Frank, hits the code button on the wall. Frank looks to the monitor: flatline.

Dr Patel, newly arrived, rushes in with a nurse's assistant:

PATEL

What's this?

ICU NURSE

He just coded.

PATEL

What a way to begin the day. Are we doing CPR? Let's give him an epinephrine, of ten milligrams. Where's the chart? Am I wrong, this is the man so long in the ER?

The nurse's assistant hands him the chart.

> (*reading*)
> Seventeen codes. That's remarkable.
> (*about Frank*)
> Who is this man?

                    ICU NURSE
> He says he's the one who brought him in.

                    PATEL
> The family?

Frank says nothing: his heart's secretly pounding.

> Seventeen codes. They must be prepared.

                    FRANK
> You know how they can be.

                    PATEL
> (*checks monitor*)
> Oh, I know. All right, that's it. I called it. Let's get some
> coffee.
> (*to Frank*)
> You going to tell the family.

Frank nods.

75. EXT. MERCY EMERGENCY – DAYBREAK

*Frank walks out of Our Lady of Perpetual Mercy, heads down the side
street. He passes Tom Wolls wielding a giant flashlight, smashing 66
Xray's headlights, denting the hood and side windows.*

                    WOLLS
> Die!

                                        CUT TO:

76. EXT. MARY'S APARTMENT BUILDING – DAY

Frank rings the buzzer. Mary, sleepy-voiced, answers:

                    MARY
                   (*O.S.*)
Who is it?

                    FRANK
Frank.

                    MARY
                   (*O.S.*)
Come on up.

                                              CUT TO:

77. INT. FIRST FLOOR – DAY

Mary, wearing a burgundy robe, opens the door. Frank says nothing.
Her expression darkens.

                    FRANK
He's dead, Mary. Your father passed.

                    MARY
                  (*avoidance*)
They moved him to ICU on the second floor.

Frank reaches out, touches her fingertips:

                    FRANK
He coded. They shocked him one too many times. I'm sorry.

She knew – for some time – this moment would come.

                    MARY
I don't know how he held up as long as he did.

                    FRANK
I'm sorry.

Frank looks at her again: it's no longer Mary, it's Rose.

                   'ROSE'
You have to keep the body going until the brain and heart
recover enough to go on.

                    FRANK
Forgive me, Rose.

'ROSE'
(Mary's voice)

It's not your fault. No one asked you to suffer. That was your idea.

FRANK

Noel was almost killed. I found him. He's going to pull through.

Mary is Mary again.

MARY

Would you like to come in?

FRANK

Yes.

Mary opens the door wider, closes it behind Frank.

CUT TO:

78. INT. MARY'S BEDROOM – DAY

Mary is Mary again: she and Frank lie clothed on her bed. He leans his head against her breast as she holds him. His eyes close: sleep.

The End

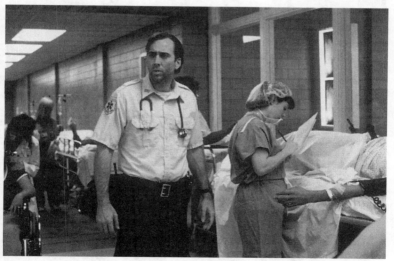

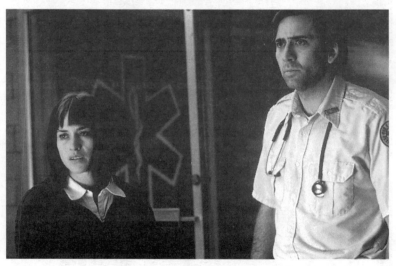